Stabilisation

By

Peter A. Prazmowski

CAMBRIDGE
SCHOLARS
PUBLISHING

Stabilisation, by Peter A. Prazmowski

This book first published 2013

Cambridge Scholars Publishing

12 Back Chapman Street, Newcastle upon Tyne, NE6 2XX, UK

British Library Cataloguing in Publication Data
A catalogue record for this book is available from the British Library

ISBN (10): 1-4438-4821-2, ISBN (13): 978-1-4438-4821-3

To my wife, my daughters, my parents and my sister

TABLE OF CONTENTS

LIST OF FIGURES

LIST OF TABLES

PREFACE

"We pay some price when necessary to bring down inflation but that price is temporary and is not large relative to the permanent gain from reduced inflation" (Martin Feldstein)

I have been unfortunate to experience, first hand, four economic crises and more than seven stabilisation attempts in my career. These have changed my perspectives on how the economy works and the way in which institutions poorly coordinated in achieving stabilisation.

The recurring elements that accompany crises, usually labelled as the *stylized facts of stabilisation*, appear inevitable and, although we have systematically learned to deal with such devastating episodes of high inflation and exchange rate devaluation, there is still much to discern about the way markets and governments manoeuvre through crisis.

How to design and implement credible and sustainable policies to stabilize inflation and exchange rates is at the heart of the literature. The essays in this book will, hopefully, contribute to our understanding of crisis and the ability to cope with the related and recurrent stylized facts of stabilisation.

The book has a technical angle that makes it appealing to academia. However, policy makers and the private sector may also find the conclusions and recommendations in the book relevant. In particular, Chapter 7 provides a summary and perhaps a quick approach to the most important findings of my research. If, however, more detail is needed, the reader may delve into the chapter that covers the topic of interest.

In editing the book, I have kept the flavour of the essays that were part of my original PhD dissertation. In this regard, many of the chapters may seem intense and the mathematics more detailed than usual. A more subtle and perhaps less comprehensive version of the chapters could be found in professional academic journals where some of the essays are either published or in the process of being published.

The reader may find the details and depth of the essays in the book engaging. I hope that the materials contained in these chapters will stimulate future research in this interesting literature that will continue to contribute to our understanding of economics in general and the economics of stabilisation in particular.

Peter Albert Prazmowski

ACKNOWLEDGMENTS

I am grateful to Dr José R. Sánchez-Fung and Professor Subrata Ghatak for their unconditional support in the long journey of putting this volume together. I would also like to express my gratitude to the *School of Economics at Kingston University* in London and its faculty for their encouragement. In particular, I would like to thank Professor Vince Daly, Dr Willy Spanjers, and Professor Peter Scott (*University of Massachusetts at Amherst*) for comments and suggestions; also Dr Joachim Stibora for useful insights, and Dr Miguel Segoviano, a dear friend from my days at the *London School of Economics*, and who is currently at the *International Monetary Fund* (IMF), for sharing interesting insights about the IMF and its current role in the global markets that helped shape many of the ideas in this book. I am in debt with Jeanet Cabrera for her assistance in this process and to many participants at Kingston PhD conferences for providing valuable feedback. Last, but not least, I would like to thank Dr Jalal Siddiki (*Kingston University*) and Dr Jose A. León-Ledesma (*Kent University*) for their time devoted on this material, enlightening comments and suggestions.

CHAPTER ONE

INTRODUCTION

Stabilisation

Economic crises arising from exchange rate volatility and high inflation have affected countries around the world and, in particular, those with developing economies. The common response of countries suffering from volatility during times of crisis has been to design and implement stabilisation packages aimed at controlling the exchange rate, stabilising inflation, and restoring economic fundamentals.

The stabilisation attempts pursued in Latin America, Israel, Turkey, and Iceland have allowed economists to identify stylized facts for each type of stabilisation strategy (e.g. Calvo and Végh 1999). The debate over which strategy to adopt for achieving stabilisation is intense, and centres on whether *exchange-rate-based stabilisation* (ERBS) programmes are superior to other types of orthodox and heterodox programmes, especially *money-based stabilisation* (MBS).

The main difference between the programmes is in the selection of the nominal anchor. ERBS uses the exchange rate, whereas MBS uses a monetary aggregate. The choice of the nominal anchor can have diverse implications. For example, Végh (1992) finds distinctive patterns in key macroeconomic variables attributed to the choice of the stabilisation strategy. The patterns are believed to influence the success of the stabilisation attempt.

Achieving the goals of stabilisation also demands financial support from institutions like the *International Monetary Fund* (IMF). The IMF assists countries in designing and implementing stabilisation programmes, and is also known for pursuing global financial and exchange rate stability through the stabilisation of inflation in countries with balance of payments difficulties. The IMF, with its role of crisis manager and lender of last resort, has generated an extensive record of stabilisation episodes, providing information for investigating the implications of IMF-supported stabilisation programmes and their corresponding stylized facts (see, for example, Fischer 1999).

The essays in this book contribute to the literature by extending some analytical models and by empirically testing their relevance across developing countries. In doing so, Chapter 2 reviews the literature on the stylized facts of stabilisation and other important concepts such as the credibility and timing of stabilisation plans. The subsequent four chapters contain original contributions to the literature on stabilisation.

One important fact of stabilisations is the drop-recovery cycle found in output and consumption during and after stabilisation programmes are implemented. The policies pursued under different stabilisation strategies will have different effects over consumption and output that could lead to regime-specific patterns. There is a substantial research programme dealing with the issue that can be classified as either demand- or supply-side approaches (see Fischer et al 2002).

Chapter 3 focuses on consumption during stabilisation. The analysis puts forward a demand-side explanation for the boom-drop cycles observed in consumption using a variation of the *stochastic life-cycle-permanent income* (SLCPI) with rational expectations model. The analysis extends Hall's (1978) model by incorporating capital mobility and currency substitution. The approach is new to the literature dealing with inflation stabilisation, and by considering a foreign currency variable, the model is also new to the SLCPI hypothesis.

The model is tested for a group of developing countries engaging in IMF supported programmes. Across this section of countries, the results reveal the significance of currency substitution and capital mobility in the SLCPI. The model is fairly successful in replicating the actual patterns of consumption during stabilisation, providing a link between consumption cycles and the ability of economic agents to hedge against devaluation and chronic inflation by shifting between currencies.

Another important stylized fact of stabilisation is the appreciation of real exchange rates after introducing ERBS programmes. There are several explanations in the literature for this phenomenon. In general, it is believed that under ERBS, inflation is slow to decline to international levels, which under a fixed nominal exchange rate will cause an appreciation of the real exchange rate. The basis for such persistence in inflation, especially under ERBS, is understood as coming from inertial forces, aggregate demand pressures and exchange rate misalignments from equilibrium. For example, Kamin (2001) explored the contribution of these sources of inflation during ERBS programmes in Mexico, and surprisingly finds that real factors, such aggregate demand pressures, are the most significant source of real exchange rate appreciation during times of crisis.

Chapter 4 investigates the behaviour of real exchange rates and inflation during stabilisation by developing a framework for changes in stabilisation preferences and credibility. The model shows that changes in preferences and credibility can lead to Lucas (1976) structural shifts, not only in the estimated inflation equations, but also at the steady state, which could caused errors in the design and implementation of the stabilisation strategy.

The econometric exercises modelling Chile's 1978 and Mexico's 1988 and 1994 stabilisation attempts endorse the theoretical framework and generate insights on the evolution of the real exchange rate and its relationship to policy preferences and credibility. In particular, the results indicate that the degree of flexibility allowed to the nominal anchor during stabilisation will have different effects over credibility and ultimately on the success of the programmes. As in Edwards (1996), credibility appears to be the fundamental force affecting the relationship between real exchange rate appreciation, inflation inertia and aggregate demand pressures.

The timing of stabilisation plans is also important. Coordination problems between the private and public sectors often delay stabilisation programmes. The key element is measuring what is known as duration in stabilisation. The literature has relied on some threshold definitions of high and low inflation for calculating the timing between the introduction of a stabilisation programme and the definitions of high and low inflation.

Chapter 5 develops and tests a model showing how policy makers decide to engage in a stabilisation programme by evaluating the variance of inflation, providing an alternative approach for measuring duration in stabilisation. The approach also gives a rationale for using Engle's (1982) *Autoregressive Conditional Herterskedasticy* (ARCH) model for empirically evaluating chronic inflation in countries with a history of stabilisation episodes. The analysis employs the volatility underlying an inflation equation as an alternative, and arguably more rigorous, threshold definition of high and low inflation in the calculation of duration.

The hypothesis is tested for a group of developing countries engaging in several IMF supported ERBS programmes. The results from the modelling show that inflation rates are heteroscedastic and that the ARCH overshoots near or on the dates the stabilisation programmes are announced. Notably, the results show no correlation between the ARCH and failed stabilisation programmes. The analysis reveals that competing frameworks like Hamman (2001) exaggerate duration and may have over-emphasised the importance of coordination problems in the timing of stabilisation plans.

The debate over choosing a nominal anchor for stabilisation is fundamentally based on the stylized facts pertinent to each type of stabilisation strategy. There is, however, a great deal of emphasis on the degree of discipline that each anchor imposes over fiscal and monetary policies and its relationship to the final choice of the nominal anchor (see Tornell and Velasco 1998). The question still lingers: can the type of nominal anchor influence the perception of agents on the effectiveness of stabilisation efforts? This is relevant as credibility may affect inflation persistence and the success of the stabilisation programme (see Agénor and Taylor 1992).

Chapter 6 examines the credibility of stabilisation programmes relying on different types of nominal anchors. The analysis uses methods advanced in the literature for calculating an approximate measure of credibility for each of the stabilisation strategies (e.g. Edwards 1998), and applies the techniques to a cross-section of countries that have undergone ERBS and MBS programmes. Armed with a panel of 19 countries registering a total of 39 stabilisation episodes, the analysis concludes that countries experiencing higher inflation persistence prior to stabilisation are more inclined to pursuing MBS than ERBS. It also reveals that ERBS are percieved as more credible than MBS. A further important finding is that the impact of stabilisation over inertia has declined since the 1970s. Additionally, it appears that the size, region, and level of development of countries engaging in stabilisation affect the likelihood of reducing inflation inertia.

Policy Implications

There are important policy implications derived from the essays that can provide a practical application to crisis and that are also summarized in Chapter 7. In particular, Chapter 3 offers advice on the potential consequences of currency substitution and capital mobility when exchange rate expectations are volatile or when local interest rates substantially depart from international levels. It also highlights the welfare implications of credit constraints on consumers that are unable to hedge or act against exchange and interest rate movements, especially during times of crisis.

Chapter 4 concludes that changes in credibility will affect the short- and long-term structural characteristic of estimated inflation models, especially during the implementation of stabilisation programmes. The results extend the Lucas (1976) critique dealing with the effects of policy reaction on econometric modelling. The conclusions have important implications for the ability of policy makers and the IMF to forecast the effects of their packages when volatility is high and expectations are changing. As a consequence, the performance of the programmes can change public perception, creating a structural bias that could mislead the authorities in the implementation of stabilisation plans.

Chapter 5, dealing with the timing of stabilisation, provides a simple and testable framework that will allow central banks and the IMF to monitor the volatility of the economy, advising on the correct time to engage in stabilisation policies. The monitoring process, using the techniques suggested by the model, allows identifying unexpected changes in the evolution of key indicators, helping to anticipate periods of crisis and, once a stabilisation package is in place, the timing when the economy regains stability.

Finally, Chapter 6 provides a set of benchmarks related to the size and level of development of countries engaging in stabilisation that could be used to suggest the correct type of stabilisation strategy. In particular, the panel highlights that ERBS programmes have a larger announcement effect on inflation persistence compared to other forms of stabilisation. However, this result changes among regions and over time depending, for example, on the popularity and success record of each type of anchor. These finds, and those that could be obtained from further research, should be useful to the IMF and to countries planning to engage in IMF-supported programmes.

Conclusion

One interesting characteristic of this literature is that it draws on many areas in economics. The review chapter provides a taste of the literature, and is divided according to each area of research pertinent to stabilisation. In this regard, the remaining chapters fall into one or several of these areas, and could be regarded as a collection of essays in the field of stabilisation.

In particular, Chapters 3 and 4 deal with the stylized facts of stabilisation. Chapter 5 deals with the timing of stabilisation and what the literature calls duration in stabilisation. The conclusions to be drawn from chapter 5 also spill over into other areas of research dealing with political opportunism and the political economy of reforms.

Finally, Chapters 4 and 6 also deal with the concept of credibility, which has become a central element in understanding the success and/or failure of stabilisation attempts. Hopefully, the models put forward in the book will promote future research that could help in our understanding of crisis and stabilisation.

References

Agénor, P. R., and M. K. Taylor, 1992, Testing for Credibility Effects, *IMF Staff Papers*, 39 (3), 545-571.

Calvo, G.A., and C.A. Végh, 1999, Inflation Stabilization and BOP Crises in Developing Countries, in Taylor, J.B. and M. Woodford, (eds.) *Handbook of Macroeconomics*, 1, 1531–1614.

Edwards, S., 1996, Exchange-Rate Anchors, Credibility and Inertia: A Tale of Two Crises, Chile and Mexico, *American Economic Review*, 86 (2), 176-180.

—. 1998, Two Crises: Inflationary Inertia and Credibility, *The Economic Journal*, 108, 665-80.

Engle, R. F., 1982, Autoregressive Conditional Heteroskedasticity with Estimates of the Variance of U.K. Inflation, *Econometrica*, 50, 987-1008.

Fischer, S., 1999, On the Need for an International Lender of Last Resort, *Journal of Economic Perspectives*, 13 (4), 85-104.

Fischer, S., R. Sahay, and C. A. Végh, 2002, Modern Hyper and High Inflations, *Journal of Economic Literature*, 40, 837-880.

Hall, R. E., 1978, Stochastic Implications of the Life-Cycle Permanent Income Hypothesis: Theory and Evidence, *Journal of Political Economy*, 89, 971-987.

Hamman, J. A., 2001, Exchange-Rate-Based Stabilisation: A Critical Look at the Stylized Facts, *IMF Staff Papers*, 48 (1), 111-138.

Kamin, S. B., 2001, Real Exchange Rates and Inflation in Exchange-Rate-Based Stabilizations: an Empirical Examination, *Journal of Development Economics*, 64, 237-253.

Lucas, R. E., 1976, Econometric Policy Evaluation: a Critique, *Carnegie-Rochester Conference Series on Public Policy*, 1, 19-46.

Tornell, A., and A. Velasco, 1998, Fiscal Discipline and the Choice of a Nominal Anchor in Stabilization, *Journal of International Economics*, 46, 1-30.

Végh, C. A., 1992, Stopping High Inflation: An Analytical Overview, *IMF Staff Papers*, 39, 629-95.

CHAPTER TWO

REVIEW OF STABILISATION

Introduction

This chapter surveys the literature on stabilisation. Firstly, the review explains stabilisation programmes and the role of the *International Monetary Fund* (IMF). Secondly, the chapter discusses the stylized facts of stabilisation and the research unveiling relevant empirical regularities. In particular, the review focuses on *exchange-rate-based stabilisation* (ERBS) and *money-based stabilisation* (MBS) programmes. The chapter also deals with the concept of credibility. Credibility and the techniques for empirically investigating its role are at the core of the literature and will be further addressed in other parts of the book. The final section deals with the timing of stabilisation, the duration of stabilisation plans, and the optimal timing of stabilisation programmes.

Stabilisation Programmes

Stabilisation programmes aim at containing inflation over and above other macroeconomic objectives. For that reason, the success or failure of these programmes is commonly measured by their ability to reduce inflation and to control inertia (Edwards 1992).[1] However, stabilising inflation demands controlling intermediate targets or anchors.

For example, ERBS programmes rely on the nominal exchange rate as the intermediate target, while MBS programmes rely on the money base or some narrower definition of money as the primary anchor.[2]

---

[1] Although inflation is the primary objective during stabilisation, other indicators are relevant. For example, the behaviour of real exchange rates is important, as they tend to overly appreciate during stabilisation. This appreciation causes the economy to lose trade competitiveness, inducing a significant degree of inflation persistence (Calvo and Vegh 1999).

[2] In principle, the fundamental difference between ERBS and MBS is the use of the exchange rate or the money base as an instrument for stabilising inflation. However, there is no such thing as a pure MBS programme, since most of them

Additionally, ERBS programmes may fix the nominal exchange rate or allow it to devalue under parity by pegging the exchange rate to an inflation rate target. One interesting example is the Mexican ERBS *Pacto* programme of 1988, in which a combination of stabilisation strategies was used. In particular, the *Pacto* had three phases. It started with a fixed nominal exchange rate in a first phase, and then allowed a devaluation that was set below expected inflation. Finally, an exchange rate band was set such that the exchange rate was allowed to move freely within the band.

The intermediate target or anchor defines the scope by which stabilisation programmes can be classified. In this regard, stabilisation has two broad dimensions. Firstly, it can include fiscal corrections in the form of austerity. Secondly, income policies such as wage-price controls may be implemented. These fiscal and income policies provide support to the stabilisation effort and are usually a key element in the success of stabilisation attempts.[3]

Turning to IMF programmes, they are known to be the most popular form of stabilisation, particularly in developing countries. In its article of agreements of the 1944 *Breton Woods Conference*, the IMF was created with the purpose of assisting countries facing severe macroeconomic imbalances while promoting global economic stability.[4] The programmes focus on fiscal austerity and tight monetary policy as instruments for stabilisation. In particular, exchange rate devaluation and credit restrictions are standard measures used by the IMF to control balance of payment problems that arise from sustained periods of high inflation.

The underlying justification for such policies follow from a monetarist prescription developed by Polack (1957), understanding that inflation is "always and everywhere a monetary phenomenon" (Friedman 1968). Since the monetary base is composed by reserves and domestic credit to public and private sectors, a restrain on credit will reduce money supply, thus bringing the balance of payments to equilibrium while stopping

---

rely on a wide mixture of policies on top of money aggregates. Nevertheless, MBS tend to differ from the ERBS programmes in the lack of an explicit *de facto* pegged exchange rate. Most of the MBS cases adopted a floating exchange rate regime. Even though the rest of the chapter will continue to use the term MBS, it might seem appropriate to refer them as non-ERBS.

[3] The importance of fiscal austerity becomes more relevant in situations of severe balance of payments misalignments. In particular, and under the implementation of MBS programmes, constraints on money supply, implied by the stabilisation attempt, must be accompanied by fiscal austerity.

[4] In the same conference, the *World Bank* was also created with the purpose of providing financing for long-term economic development projects.

inflation. In addition, countries impose conditionalities that describe the necessary requirements to receive financial assistance from the IMF, other collateral lending organizations such as the *International Development Bank* and *World Bank*, as well as debt rescheduling facilities with international lenders such as the *Paris Club* (Goldstein 2000).[5]

Since its inauguration, the IMF has assisted around 189 countries with programmes that vary greatly in form and substance. For example, the IMF provides short-term assistance under a *stand-by* agreement, usually repayable within five years, under programmes aimed at providing solutions to balance of payment problems. In addition, there are extended *fund facility* programmes, established in 1974, aimed at providing medium -term assistance of two to three years, with a ten-year repayment schedule to countries facing severe imbalances in production, trade and prices.

There are also *structural adjustment facility* programmes, in which resources are made available on a concessional basis, providing medium-term macroeconomic and structural support for countries facing severe balance of payment problems. Finally, the *enhanced structural adjustment facility* is aimed at strengthening structural policies with access to funds and monitoring procedures that vary substantially (see Mussa and Savastano 1999).

In addition to IMF programmes, there are also heterodox stabilisation strategies. On top of the traditional fiscal and monetary prescriptions of the IMF, heterodox programmes rely on discretionary income policies such as wage-price and exchange rate controls.[6] Examples of heterodox stabilisation include Argentina, Bolivia, Brazil and Israel during 1985 and 1986. These countries experienced high rates of inflation and opted for discretion instead of an IMF set of measures. The programmes failed utterly in Brazil and Argentina, although inflation did stabilize in Israel and Bolivia. Research has focused on identifying the role of income policies in the success of stabilisation programmes and the ability of governments to implement reforms that are not under the scope of the IMF (for a survey of the literature on stabilisation see Bruno et al 1990). If heterodox policies fail, however, experience shows that countries usually rush to the IMF as the last hope towards stabilisation.

In addition to orthodox-IMF and heterodox programmes, stabilisation can be implemented in a gradual or shock fashion. The latter type of programme, referred to as shock therapy, became very common during the reform of the transition economies of central Europe in the 1990s. One

---

[5] See Marchesi (2003) for an analysis of the correlation between IMF programmes and the granting of debt rescheduling facilities.

[6] IMF programmes usually adopt wage restraints instead of price controls.

widely studied case is Poland's shock therapy programme of 1990, which had the objective of liberalising the economy, causing a significant drop in real output (Lipton and Sachs 1990). Under a shock therapy programme, the implementation of income policies around the nominal anchor may be so dramatic that the economy goes into a resting mode with a severe recession. In this situation, the slow-down in economic activity helps to contain inflation. However, this severe negative welfare effect is one of the reasons why shock programmes are less popular (Agénor and Montiel 1999).

Nonetheless, some positive arguments in favour of shock programmes have been posed: firstly, shock reforms motivate the reallocation of resources, lowering adjustment costs (Mussa 1984). Secondly and due to their decisive nature, these types of programme tend to enhance credibility (Hiemenz et al 1992). Thirdly, it is more feasible to establish rapid reforms provided that design of a detailed sequence of reforms is almost impossible to implement (Funke 1993). Finally, gradual reforms may deter the efficient allocation of resources (Murphy et al 1992) and may inhibit the liberalisation of the economy (Lipton and Sachs 1990).

On the contrary, gradual programmes tend to implement a set of income policies around the nominal anchor that are subtler, and usually compensate for their adverse effects on low-income sectors by using, for example, focalized subsidy mechanisms. Many countries, such as China and Japan have experienced gradual-based transitions. Other examples include the case of Chile in 1983, with an orthodox-gradual programme, while a heterodox-gradual case is the Brazilian 1964-1967 Campos-Bulhoes programme. On the other hand, heterodox-shock programmes may include, for example, the Argentina, Bolivia, Brazil and Israel programmes during 1985 and 1986, as mentioned above.

The choice of programmes and the IMF as a lender of last resort are profoundly controversial and have raised a great deal of research on the subject (see, for example, Fischer 1999). The debate has centred on the *structuralist* view, which favours heterodox type programmes versus the *monetarists'* school, which provides the essence of IMF-orthodox-gradual recipes.

The *structuralist*, and more recently the *neo-structuralist*, argue that IMF packages impose an unnecessary burden on society, leading to losses in output, growth and employment. For example, regarding the IMF prescription for devaluating the currency, Dornbusch (1973) shows that under fixed international prices, such policies lower aggregate demand. Cooper (1971) also argues that if the initial trade deficit is very large, a devaluation that improves the trade balance may have adverse aggregate demand effects.

Diaz-Alejandro (1963) points out that any given devaluation may cause aggregate demand to fall if a significant redistributing effect is induced. This effect increases the income of capitalists and reduces the income of workers, under the assumption that workers have a greater propensity to consume. Ahmed (1986) also shows that if the country has a substantial foreign debt and if *purchasing power parity* (PPP) does not strictly hold, devaluation will increase the debt burden and will therefore lower aggregate demand.

In addition, Krugman and Taylor (1978) show that under large trade deficits, if exports and imports react slowly to prices, a devaluation of the exchange rate will, in the short run, increase domestic spending above earnings from exports and, therefore, cause aggregate demand and non-tradable production to fall. Other authors argue that aggregate supply will fall during devaluations due to increases in import prices of raw materials, increases in wages that are linked to exchange rate expectations and increases in interest rates due to a fall in money supply associated with the devaluation of the exchange rate (Van Wijnbergen 1986).

There is also research showing a contractionary effect from credit restraints. If financial markets are underdeveloped, the banking system becomes a firm's only source of financing. A credit restraint will raise interest rates, reducing investment and aggregate output (van Wijnbergen 1983). Credit restraint may also increase the opportunity cost of capital, limiting the availability of credit, thus lowering aggregate supply (Bruno 1979).

On a global basis, Williamson (1981) has argued that if credit restrains are applied simultaneously to a group of countries in the form of stabilisation, a worldwide recession may occur, affecting the ex-post performance of the countries under the programme. Therefore, according to the *structuralists*, devaluation and credit restraints provide no immediate solution to balance of payment problems or to economic crisis.

In defence of their structural packages, the IMF argues that corrective measures are necessary to avoid a more painful medicine down the road. However, some authors have suggested that excessive conditionalities required by the IMF create concerns regarding the ability of governments to commit to the programmes (Goldstein 2000). Nonetheless, the IMF argues that their corrective measures are the best antidote to balance of payment problems (Nowzad 1981). Other empirical studies have suggested that conditionalities have negligible additional effects over economic growth, as they reflect government policies that would have been implemented regardless of the IMF programme (Dreher 2006). The IMF has also argued that their stabilisation packages promote aggregate supply through policies orientated towards reducing price distortions and trade barriers (see, for instance, Khan and Knight 1982). Finally, the IMF understands that most of the *structuralists*' arguments are already incorporated in their stabilisation packages.

Although at the theoretical level the debate has remained unresolved, at the empirical level evidence shows strong support for IMF programmes. For example, Gylfason (1987) compares the macroeconomic performance of developing countries on IMF stabilisation packages against countries with similar balance of payments difficulties, but without formal programmes. He finds strong support for the IMF in terms of controlling inflation and improving the balance of payments without significant negative effects over output performance.[7]

Stylized Facts of Stabilisation

The stabilisations pursued in Latin America, Israel, Turkey, and Iceland attempting to alleviate chronic inflation, have allowed establishing important stylized facts. Calvo and Végh (1999) and more recently Fischer et al (2002), have established facts regarding the choice of nominal anchors. Table 2.1 presents the most relevant.

Table 2.1: Empirical regularities of stabilisation programmes

Exchange-rate-based stabilisation	Money-based stabilisation
1. Slow convergence of the inflation rate to the devaluation rate	1. Slow convergence of the inflation rate to the rate of growth of the money supply
2. Real appreciation of the domestic currency	2. Real appreciation of the domestic currency
3. Initial increase in real GDP and private consumption followed by later contraction	3. Initial contraction in economic activity

Source: Calvo and Végh (1999)

[7] One important aspect of stabilisation that has recently being explored is the credibility effect induced by IMF packages (see Bird 2002). It is believed that IMF conditionalities are more credible than discretion, thus raising the ex-post success probability of the programmes.

Facts one and two, which are common across programmes, imply that the nominal exchange rate decelerates faster than domestic prices, resulting in a real appreciation of the exchange rate. A literature has emerged trying to understand the reasons behind the real appreciation of the exchange rate, taking two broad approaches.

The first focuses on a framework that assumes that the real exchange rate starts out at a steady state level prior to stabilisation and that several aspects of the programmes cause a subsequent appreciation. The second shows that as a result of internal and external misalignments, the real exchange rate starts out away from equilibrium and converges to the steady state after stabilisation policies are implemented.

Within the former framework, however, there are two potential explanations for the observed behaviour of the real exchange rate. One understands that various aspects of stabilisation lead to higher aggregate demand, raising non-tradable prices and causing a real appreciation of the currency. Calvo and Végh (1993) argue that if stabilisation is not credible, consumers will increase spending while conditions remain stable. Uribe (1995) and Roldos (1995) view inflation as a tax that, when reduced through stabilisation, will boost investment and consumption, causing an appreciation of the real exchange rate. Rebelo and Végh (1995) highlight that fiscal reforms associated with stabilisation programmes reduce the need for distortion financing, increasing permanent income, leading to higher consumption and a lower real exchange rate. Finally, Erceg and Levin (1996) argue that the structural reforms in most stabilisation programmes increase the desired capital stock, leading to higher output and a lower real exchange rate.

Under the second set of explanations, inflation is slow to decline to international levels due to overlapping contracts, imperfect credibility, and backward-looking expectations that, under a fixed nominal exchange rate anchor, lead to an appreciation of the real exchange rate. Rodríguez (1982) uses a model of non-tradable inflation that assumes that expected inflation adjusts sluggishly to changes in actual inflation. In Dornbusch and Werner (1994), inflation depends on wage growth, which is determined by expected inflation and approximated by lagged inflation. In the last two cases, with a fixed nominal exchange rate, sticky prices cause a real appreciation of the currency. In Edwards (1996), wage growth depends on the credibility of the stabilisation programme. If the programme is not fully credible and the nominal exchange rate is anchored, non-tradable inflation resulting from wage inertia leads to a real appreciation of the currency.

The final explanation argues that domestic inflation is linked to the gap between the real exchange rate and its equilibrium or steady state level.

Due to balance-of-payments misalignments and a highly devalued nominal exchange rate prior to stabilisation, the real exchange rate may be away from its domestic market-clearing level, causing pressures on non-tradable prices. Again, under a nominal exchange rate anchor, inflation persistence will cause an appreciation of the real exchange rate until equilibrium is restored (see Kamin 2001; Gil-Diaz and Carstens 1996). Kamin (2001) finds that inflation in Mexico is mostly driven by these type of real exchange rate misalignments.[8]

According to fact three in Table 2.1, however, the most salient difference between the two types of stabilisation strategies is the real effect over economic activity and the business cycle. In particular, ERBS exhibits a consumption boom early in the programme followed by a contraction, whereas MBS exhibits an initial consumption drop followed by a recovery. The literature exploring these boom-drop-recovery cycles, known as the *recession-now-versus-recession-later* hypotheses, uses models aimed at replicating the empirical regularities in consumption following stabilisation.

There are four main explanations in the literature aimed at capturing such consumption patterns (see Fischer et al 2002). An earlier explanation, originally presented by Rodríguez (1982) following Cagan (1956), was based on backward-looking inflation expectations. Accordingly, if there are backward-looking expectations, and *uncovered interest parity* (UIP) holds such that nominal interest rates fall proportionally with the exchange rate, real interest rates will fall. As a result, consumption will increase.

These models provide a good explanation for episodes in which real interest rates fall early in the programme like the Argentine 1978 plan. However, they cannot explain programmes in which real interest rates suddenly increase due to the implementation of stabilisation policies, such as many heterodox attempts in the mid-1980s (see Calvo and Végh 1999).

Calvo and Végh (1999), and Calvo (1986) are examples of models that explain consumption boom-drop cycles using the *temporariness hypothesis*. According to their explanation, under ERBS the exchange rate is not usually a fully credible anchor implying that consumers, perceiving its temporariness, anticipate a future devaluation. Acting on this perception, agents increase consumption of tradable goods and services. However, as

---

[8] One merit of Kamin's approach is that it successfully combines both equilibrium and inertial theories in an *error correction model* (ECM) that allows identifying the contribution of each explanation to the real appreciation of the exchange rate. One limitation of the model, however, is its light theoretical substance in the development of the partial adjustment ECM formulation.

the economy stabilizes and the anchor consolidates, the process creates an eventual slowdown.

Figure 2.1a: Log changes in an average real exchange rate index (MBS)

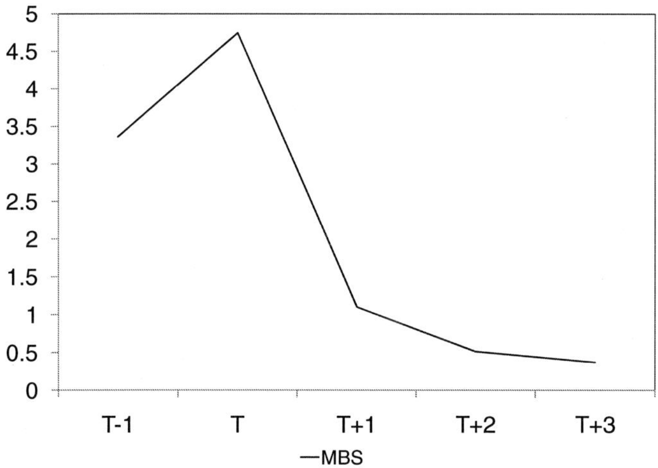

Figure 2.1b: Log changes in an average real exchange rate index (ERBS)

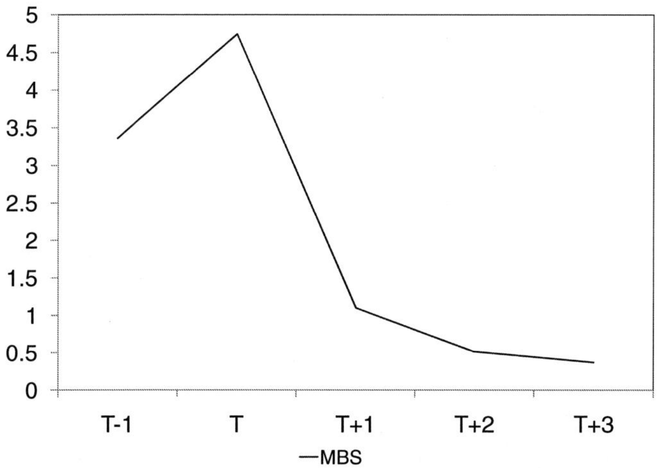

Figure 2.2a: Average GDP growth (MBS)

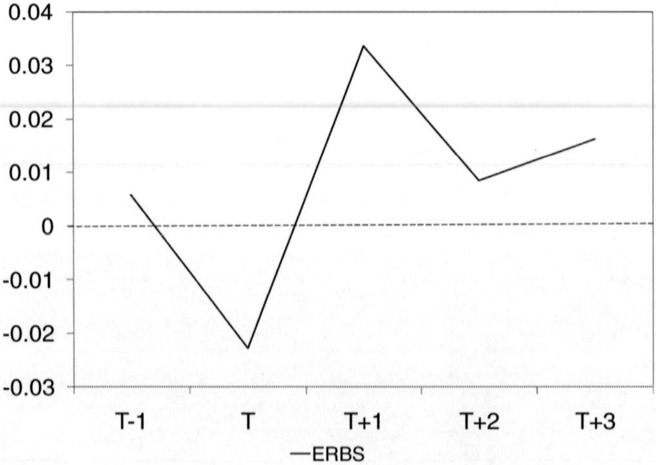

Figure 2.2b: Average GDP growth (ERBS)

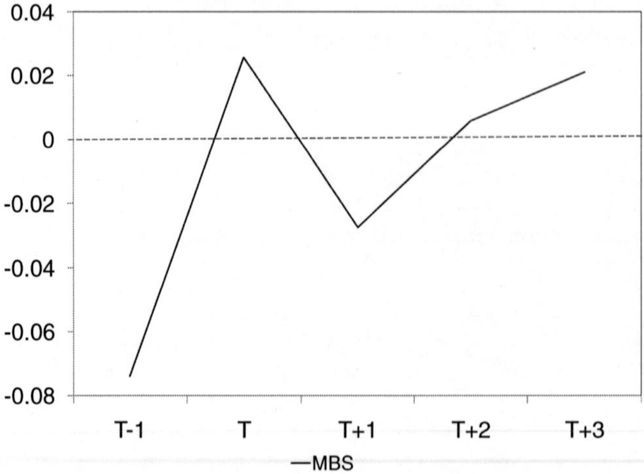

In an attempt to provide a comparison between both types of programmes, (Calvo 2007) also studies MBS programmes under the assumption of imperfect credibility. He also finds that MBS programmes lead to higher interest rates and lower output relative to ERBS ones. There are two potential problems with this hypothesis, however. Firstly, it can only explain consumption booms in non-credible programmes. Secondly, and most importantly, the hypothesis relies heavily on a large elasticity of substitution in consumption, which has been found unlikely (Reinhart and Végh 1995).

De Gregorio et al (1998) provide a related explanation. In their model, consumption follows an inventory (*S,s*) type rule for the purchase of durable, non-tradable, goods.[9] Under the assumption that stabilisation generates a wealth-income effect, unplanned consumption will be carried forward creating an early boom that, as inventories are replenished, will be followed by a later contraction. One important aspect of the model is that it can reproduce a boom-drop cycle without using credibility as the central argument. The above explanations can be classified as demand-side approaches mainly focusing on demand driven factors.

A fourth and final explanation, which is a supply-side view, treats inflation as a tax on either income or labour. This tax will affect the consumption-leisure choice, which under a stabilisation programme will create an early boom in consumption. The boom is created since many of the policies implemented under the stabilisation programme reduce the tax effect when inflation is stabilized. This view, however, is not capable of generating the different consumption patterns observed during ERBS and MBS programmes (see Lahiri, 2000 and 2001; and Rebelo and Végh, 1995). An additional way of looking at these stylized facts is through graphical representation. Figures 2.1a and 2.1b show the log changes in the cross sectional average of a real exchange rate index for a group of developing countries that have undergone IMF stabilisation programmes.[10]

The evolution of the real exchange rate captures facts one and two in Table 2.1, which under both MBS and ERBS programmes, tend to fall due to a slow convergence of local inflation to international levels and/or an appreciation of the nominal exchange rate. As it is evident from the charts,

---

[9] The (S, s) inventory management model is characterized by a bandwidth of inventory with a lower limit designated as s and an upper limit designated as S. When inventory levels fall below s, agents purchase enough inventories to raise the levels to S. When inventories lie within the band, no action is taken. The seminal work suggesting endogenous inventory cycles is Meltzer (1941) and the conventional wisdom on the use of inventories as buffer to smooth cycles follows from Holt et al (1960). A survey on inventory and (S, s) type rules can be found in Blinder and Maccini (1991).

[10] In the graphs, the year of stabilisation is labelled T and the average is carried out according to the actual dates of stabilisation for each country in the sample. Table 2.2 presents the countries and dates of stabilisation used in the construction of the graphs.

the real exchange rates in both cases tend to appreciate on average during and after the programmes are introduced.

It is also interesting to see that the real exchange rate appears to start out more depreciated under MBS than under ERBS. Some authors like Kamin (2001) suggest that the real exchange rate starts out more depreciated than a market clearing equilibrium level. As inflation persists, the real exchange rate appreciates until equilibrium is restored. According to the charts, it appears that the gap might be larger under MBS than under ERBS.

Additionally, Figures 2.2a and 2.2b show the cross-section average of growth of real GDP for the sample countries. Under ERBS, GDP falls in the first year of the programme and then recovers in the second and third year. Under MBS, GDP booms in the first year of the programme and drops in the third and fourth year after it is introduced. The fall is sometimes in the magnitude of negative growth, and is one of the reasons the literature dealing with these drop-recovery patterns is usually referred to as *recession-now-versus-recession-later* hypothesis.

Stabilisation and Inflation Inertia

Strong inertial forces have predominantly characterized inflation in developing countries. Inertia implies that today's inflation depends on past-realized levels, and as a consequence shocks will be passed on to future prices through inflation persistent. Therefore, it becomes vital to understand the fundamental drivers behind inertia in order to effectively design policies aimed at achieving stylization.

According to Dornbusch and Simonsen (1988), the inflation process can be represented by a combination of excess demand forces capturing economic overheating when reaching some structural bottleneck, random exogenous supply shocks hitting the economy in a favourable or adverse fashion (e.g. changes in international oil price, natural catastrophes, etc.), and inflation persistence.

The reason for such persistence or inertia is understood to be result of some sort of formal or informal indexation. During times of crisis, it is common to find wage rules that are legally binding in setting wage increases, as well as informal wage bargains aimed at compensating for past inflation. There are also expectation mechanisms that create inertial effects. For example, firms may set prices according to increases in costs, and marketing strategies followed by competitors that most likely reflect the performance of past inflation.

Table 2.2: IMF stabilisation country, date and anchor type

Country	Region	Beginning Date	Exchange Rate Anchor
Argentina 1	Latin America	1976	MBS
Argentina 2	Latin America	1980	ERBS
Argentina 3	Latin America	1985	ERBS
Argentina 4	Latin America	1991	ERBS
Bolivia	Latin America	1985	MBS
Brazil 1	Latin America	1965	ERBS
Brazil 2	Latin America	1990	MBS
Chile 1	Latin America	1964	MBS
Chile 2	Latin America	1974	MBS
Chile 3	Latin America	1977	ERBS
Costa Rica	Latin America	1982	MBS
Dominican Republic 1	Caribbean	1985	MBS
Dominican Republic 2	Caribbean	1991	MBS
Ecuador	Latin America	1983	MBS
Ecuador	Latin America	1984	MBS
Ecuador	Latin America	1988	MBS
Ecuador	Latin America	1992	ERBS
Iceland	Other	1976	MBS
Iceland	Other	1983	ERBS
Israel	Other	1985	ERBS
Jamaica	Caribbean	1992	MBS
Mexico	Latin America	1983	MBS
Mexico	Latin America	1987	ERBS
Mexico	Latin America	1995	ERBS
Nicaragua	Latin America	1991	ERBS
Nigeria	Other	1990	MBS
Nigeria	Other	1993	MBS
Peru	Latin America	1985	ERBS
Peru	Latin America	1990	MBS
Turkey	Other	1980	MBS
Turkey	Other	1999	ERBS
Uganda	Other	1981	MBS
Uganda	Other	1988	MBS
Uruguay	Latin America	1969	ERBS
Uruguay	Latin America	1975	MBS
Uruguay	Latin America	1980	ERBS
Uruguay	Latin America	1990	ERBS
Venezuela	Latin America	1989	MBS
Zambia	Other	1993	MBS

Sources: Haman (2001), Easterly (1996), Torn ell and Velasco (1998), IFS and National Sources
Note: MBS group all types of programmes that do not have an explicit nominal anchor. In this regard, the more accurate connotation would be non-ERBS programmes. We have kept MBS for expositional purposes.

In any case, as a result of inertia, inflation expectations are based on the notion that inflation tomorrow will almost certainly be above today's inflation, unless some policy or exogenous event is expected to occur. As a consequence, wage and price increases will be granted, creating a self-fulfilling process that generates additional inflation (Pazos 1972).

There are numerous ways of formally introducing inertia in an inflation model. For example, there are overlapping or staggered contracts (Calvo 1983), backward-looking expectations in setting wages and prices (Dornbusch and Werner 1994), and imperfect credibility over policy (Calvo and Végh 1993). On the other hand, inertial inflation can also be the result of policy feedback rules introduced by the authorities.

In many developing countries, central banks usually follow policies aimed at accommodating the value of the exchange rate in order to maintain or improve the country's trade performance in terms of its relative international competitiveness. These rules, called *crawling peg* regimes, periodically adjust the nominal or "spot" exchange rate according to past price differentials between the country and its main trading partner, thus creating an inertial effect (see Williamson, 1981).

Edwards (1992), for example, developed a model which is a variant of Dornbusch's (1980) tradable/non-tradable framework originally pioneered by Salter (1959) and Swan (1960), and which captures the salient features of developing countries, especially in Latin America. In this framework, inertia could be present, even under rational forward-looking wage expectations with no formal or informal indexation, as a result of the rules implemented in the conduct of exchange rate policy. In addition, Edwards (1996) shows that credibility on the stabilisation policies plays a determinant role in the evolution of inflation inertia and in the design and implementation of stabilisation policies.

Credibility and Stabilisation Policies

The literature on stabilisation argues that credibility on a programme can reduce the cost of disinflation by changing the expectations about the future path of inflation through its role in the setting of wage and price decisions (Taylor 1982). In contrast, when stabilisation policies lack credibility, the public may recognize that the programme will not be maintained and collectively cause it to collapse.

There are arguments and evidence for the importance of credibility and its role on the potential opportunity costs of stabilisation policies. The subject was formally developed in Dornbusch and Fisher (1986); however,

Sargent (1982) shows that depending on the level of credibility stabilisation can be implemented with little or no output costs as was evident during the hyperinflation episodes of Austria, Germany, Poland and Hungary after World War I. Closely related to Sargent's approach, is Persson and Tabellini's (1990) game-theoretic framework for analysing the concept of credibility within the context of central bankers and policy makers. If agents perceive that a new stabilisation regime will be abandoned, the structural properties of inflation will not change and persistence will remain. If there is full credibility on the programme, however, inertial inflation will disappear and inflation will be driven by aggregate misalignments and exogenous supply shocks. In this case, inflation will be fully controlled and the stabilisation programme can be regarded as successful (see Edwards 1998).

In contrast, Taylor (1975) argues that even if stabilisation programmes are fully credible, the speed at which inflation can be reduced may be slow because the public will only gradually learn about the new stabilisation environment. Hence, in countries that suffer from persistent high inflation, stabilisation can be costly regardless of the level of credibility, as inertial forces are already built in the dynamics of economic fundamentals, taking longer for agents to incorporate the new set stabilisation rules.

In addition, credibility in a stabilisation programme has an "announcement" and an "implementation" effect. The announcement effect measures the initial credibility shock that the programme might have over relevant nominal and real variables. On the other hand, the implementation effect measures the evolution of credibility as the stabilisation attempt consolidates. Both of these effects, however, respond to factors such as the consistency of fiscal and monetary policy, asymmetric information regarding policy instruments, and uncertainty regarding the economic environment.

First of all, credibility on the stabilisation programme can be affected by the inconsistencies among the policies that are simultaneously implemented. For instance, disinflation policies under a nominal anchor require the use of restrictive fiscal policy. If stabilisation is not followed by controls on public spending, agents will doubt that the programme will be sustained, causing a loss of confidence in the policies and a potential collapse of the programme (see, for example, Auernheimer 1987).

Lack of credibility can also be the result of time inconsistencies in the stabilisation package. If agents understand that the government has an incentive to deviate ex-post from the stabilisation effort in order to derive output gains once expectations are set at a lower inflation level, the programmes will lack credibility even before the stabilisation attempt is implemented (Barro and Gordon 1983).

Only in situations in which there are proper institutional arrangements such as independent central bankers (Rogoff 1985) or if there exists a reputation equilibrium for commitment (Barro 1986), and the existence of contracts such as an IMF programme or Walsh (1995) type contracts that ensure ex-post stabilisation policies will be maintained, will the credibility source be of relevance.[11] As shown in Cukierman (1991), the incentive to inflate can be the result not only of the Phillips (1958) trade-off between inflation and unemployment, or the trade-off between inflation and output (Okun 1962), but also due to short term rigidities in taxes, the need to reduce the real value of the government debt, or to increase the international competitiveness of the country through the terms of trade.

A third source of credibility problems comes from incomplete or asymmetric information regarding the true objectives of the government during stabilisation. It is common to find governments that may not be serious about their attempts to stabilize inflation even under the restrictions imposed by the IMF. This incomplete source of information will challenge the credibility of the programme and is perhaps one of the primary reasons why stabilisation attempts frequently fail. Evidence of such a situation can be found in the 1996 *Cruzado Plan*, the *Bresser Plan* of 1987 in Brazil (Agénor and Taylor 1992), and the several failed MBS stabilisation attempts in the Dominican Republic between 2003 and 2004 (Sánchez-Fung 2005).

There is also Poole's (1970) instrument uncertainty, in which the public may understand that the government has an imperfect control of the anchor. This source of uncertainty will cause agents to lose confidence in the ability of the government to effectively carry out the stabilisation attempt (see Agénor and Bhandari 1991).[12] In addition, there is uncertainty regarding the ability of agents to predict the possible outcomes of stabilisation. Since projections are done in a stochastic environment, external shocks may be large enough to throw the stabilisation plan off track, causing a loss of confidence on the programme. Hence, agents may perceive that the programme's success probability will be low if

---

[11] It can be argued that time inconsistencies may not affect downward the *announcement* effect of the programmes, if these programmes are implemented under the surveillance of an international body such as IMF.

[12] Their model concentrates on the implication of lack of government spending control and its relationship to the probability of collapse of the stabilisation programme.

uncertainty is high and will lose credibility in the ability to successfully achieve disinflation (see Flood 1983).[13]

Finally, there is a less direct but related issue regarding the reputation of a government for controlling inflation. This reputation effect can be more pronounced during the introduction than during the implementation of the programme, in which the mere announcement of a stabilisation package implemented by a newly elected government may induce an initial credibility shock that can be effective in reducing inflation inertia.

Although all of these are important concepts for understanding the links between credibility and disinflation policies, at the empirical level it is difficult to isolate which source of credibility is being affected. Few studies have tried to separate the sources of credibility problems (see, for example, Bordo and Redish 1990) and most empirical tests focus on the issues as a whole. However, it is reasonable to argue that within the announcement effect at the time of stabilisation, time inconsistency, uncertainty and reputation may be the main sources of credibility problems.

As a way forward, a strand of the literature has focussed on ways of measuring credibility and to evaluate the factors affecting its evolution before and after stabilisation programmes are introduced. For example, Ágenor and Taylor (1992) developed a two-step approach, using a proxy of a credibility variable by means of the *Kalman* filter, to test for credibility effects during the *Cruzado* stabilisation plan implemented in Brazil. The approach revealed that inertial inflation is affected by credibility. Subsequently, Prazmowski (2002) extended Agénor and Taylor (1992), testing how government policy and reforms might influence ex-post credibility, and, as a consequence, the long-term success of a stabilisation programme. Knot et al (1998) also show that credibility is directly related to fiscal and monetary misalignments and their effects over the success of stabilisation programmes.

The Nominal Anchor

The literature on stabilisation is concerned with the selection of the nominal anchor when engaging in any stabilisation attempt. The debate is centred on whether ERBS is superior to other forms of stabilisation, especially MBS programmes (Calvo and Vegh 1994). The selection of the nominal anchor is usually carried out by evaluating the stylized facts pertinent to each type of anchor and by assessing their welfare implications.

[13] In Flood's (1983) model, agents' anticipation of a possible future abandonment of the stabilisation programme creates a self-fulfilling process.

As presented in section 2.3, exchange rate pegs are characterized by an expansion of real economic activity in the early stages of the programme, followed by a decline at the late stages of the stabilisation attempt. Under MBS programmes, however, the opposite pattern is common, with a drop kicking in at the beginning of the programmes and followed by a recovery in real economic activity. Despite some mixed evidence (see Hamman 2001; Easterly 1996), the stabilisation attempts in the last four decades have left a legacy of cases that support these mayor-stylized facts (Calvo and Vegh 1999). The conventional wisdom remains, however, that the cost in terms of output losses will be paid up front under MBS, whereas under ERBS these costs will be postponed.

Choosing programmes based on whether the costs of stabilisation are borne at the beginning or later in the programmes relates to the *recession-now-versus-recession-later* hypothesis. In this regard, the choice of the nominal anchor takes into consideration the output cost of deflation and is based on the sacrifice ratio resulting from the two alternative strategies. For example, Fischer (1986), based on the sacrifice ratio, concludes that ERBS programmes should be the preferred stabilisation strategy.[14] Chadha et al (1992) also conclude that ERBS cuts this ratio in half compared to a money anchor. These views are influenced by the staggered-contract approach of Fischer (1977) and Taylor (1979, 1980). Under these models, contracts are assumed to remain present for a number of consecutive periods, introducing price persistence. These models are based on the assumption that the credibility is not enough to mitigate the cost of deflation.

At the empirical level, however, money anchors are less common than exchange rate pegs. This revealed preference for choosing ERBS over MBS may be rationalized on a number of grounds, all of which suggest that ERBS should be the preferred form of stabilisation strategy (see Calvo and Vègh 1999). One concern against the use of ERBS and in favour of MBS is in situations of low credibility and/or high volatility.

---

[14] These ideas have also influenced a new literature in which the programmes are chosen based on the political gains that governments derived from the timing and the cost of each type of stabilisation strategy. Since ERBS programmes create an initial boom followed by a contraction, whereas MBS ones generate a burst followed by a recovery, policy-makers may consider the timing of elections when determining the nominal anchor for stabilisation. Aisen (1994) finds strong evidence that the choice of nominal anchor depends on elections, implying the existence of political opportunism. In particular, ERBS programmes are, on average, launched before elections while MBS ones are introduced after elections.

Theory suggests that imperfect credibility has dramatically different consequences under each type of nominal anchor (see Calvo and Vègh 1994). Under ERBS, lack of credibility is more disruptive because it reduces inflation by less and at the same time increases the size of the cycles in real economic activity (i.e. volatility). In contrast, lack of credibility in MBS reduces both the benefits of stabilisation in terms of lower inflation as well as the cost in terms of the initial recession. Hence, as pointed out in Calvo and Végh (1999) "if the public is sceptical, a money anchor may be less risky".[15]

Optimal Anchors and the Timing of Stabilisation

There is an extensive literature, pioneered by the earlier works of Tinbergen (1952), dealing with the choice of optimal policies under uncertainty. This line of research deals with problems in which a social planner chooses instruments, reforms and/or regimes according to the first and second moments of their economic environment. For example, the central bank may evaluate the welfare implications of alternative policy instruments, selecting those that minimize social losses under specific model assumptions.

Following some historical accounts of the literature, Poole (1970) in his seminal contribution analysed the question of whether the central bank should target money stock or the interest rate, showing that the selection of the optimal instrument should be made based on the relative variance of its targets. Brainard (1967), for example, was concerned with the use of fiscal or monetary policy when the authorities are uncertain about their impact on economic activity. He shows that the selection should be based on the instrument or policy with the lowest variance. Within the context of the open economy, Friedman (1968) examined the circumstances under which flexible exchange rates are optimal, while Boyer (1978) proposed the most beneficial exchange-rate regime under imperfect information.[16]

---

[15] It is also argued that ERBS programmes induce more fiscal discipline than MBS programmes, translating into greater credibility and a higher success probability. However, Tornell and Velasco (1998) showed that the experience in Latin America, with the exception of Mexico and Brazil, says otherwise. In fact, they relate the degree of impatience of the policy maker with the degree of fiscal discipline. If policy makers are inpatient, then MBS programmes will provide more discipline and perhaps greater credibility than ERBS ones.

[16] Other important contributions to this debate include Friedman (1953) and Mundell (1963).

Subsequently, and within the literature on rules versus discretion, Barro and Gordon (1983) assessed the dynamic inconsistency of monetary policy that creates an inflation bias, and modelled the optimal response of the central bank accordingly. Rogoff (1985) evaluated the trade-off between low average inflation and policy flexibility in response to shocks, suggesting the delegation of monetary policy to a conservative central banker in order to improve social welfare.

In the above models, the choice of instruments, regimes and/or reforms depend on the variance of the shock to the system. A natural extension of this literature deals with the optimal timing of regime changes, in which a switch of regime is triggered by their relative volatility (see, for example, Flood and Marion 1994). Within the literature on stabilisation, the optimal anchor is usually defined based on the ability of the anchor to bring down inflation with minimum real associated costs (see Tornell and Velasco 1998).

Another important aspect is the timing of stabilisation. For instance, Fischer (1999) has noted that governments avoid implementing IMF programmes and usually delay too long over introducing a stabilisation strategy. There is a literature on the timing of stabilisation taking two broad approaches. One revolves around a political business cycle in which the timing of the programme is based on the political and economic gains associate with stabilisation (see, for example, Sturzenegger and Tommasi 1998).

The second approach focuses on the optimal timing from an empirical perspective. For example, Flood and Marion (1994) relate the optimal timing of a regime switch to the point at which the relative variance of the stochastic shocks triggers a switching rule. At the practical level, however, there is little evidence on the performance of the rules against actual data. Most of the empirical literature draws from models that analyze the factors that explain regime changes, unable to determine if the direction and timing of the switch is optimal.

A further empirical question is whether governments adopting the regime switch behave according to the prescription of the models. Veiga, (2002) studies the effect of IMF loans on stabilisation. He finds that high political fragmentation has a significant delaying effect, but is unable to establish if the loan itself has consequences on the timing of stabilisation.

A related subject is what the literature calls “duration” in stabilisation. There are two types of duration: The first, known as “delays” in stabilisation, measures the time between the dates in which the economy reaches a threshold definition of high inflation and the date the authorities implement a formal stabilisation programme. The second, known as a "stabilisation episode", is the length between the date the authorities implement the programme and the date in which the economy reaches some definition of inflation stability. The first type of duration provides an assessment of the agility of the authorities when engaging in stabilisation and the second measures the effectiveness of the programme in controlling inflation.

The literature dealing with duration in stabilisation focuses on the externalities and political games that cause policy makers to delay stabilisation and/or to implement soft programmes that ultimately fail. For example, Alesina and Drazen (1991) argue that delays in fiscal stabilisation result from the failure of rival interest groups to agree on a deficit reduction programme. This situation leads to a war of attrition in which an agreement to engage in a stabilisation programme is only reached when one of the groups accepts paying a higher proportion of the stabilisation cost.

Drazen and Grilli (1993) extended the argument by emphasizing the possible benefits of economic crises. Since higher costs of delays rush stabilisations by revealing the looser preferences, an exogenous shock that worsens economic conditions may be welfare improving if the costs are compensated by the benefits of earlier stabilisation. Laban and Sturzenegger (1994b) show that class conflicts between the rich and the poor and their adjustment costs lead to delays in stabilisations within the context of the Latin American debt crisis.

In Laban and Sturzenegger (1994a) delays occur due to higher costs of stabilisation, lower costs of inflation, and/or lower costs of financial adaptation. Mondino, Sturzenegger and Tommasi (1996) extend this framework by incorporating the possibility of recurrent cycles of inflation and stabilisation. Fernandez and Rodrik (1991) illustrate how voters may reject reforms that would benefit the majority of the population when the identity of the gainers cannot be determined before the programme is introduced.

At the empirical level, however, the testable implications of these theories rely on measures of duration. The standard approach for measuring duration is by the difference between the date of stabilisation and the time when an economy reaches some threshold definition of high and low inflation. Ball (1994) and Easterly (1996) have used rules for defining stabilisation episodes. For example, Easterly (1996) proposes a measure of duration in which an inflation crisis is defined as a period of at least two consecutive years of inflation above 40 per cent, and a stabilisation episode, as a movement from an inflation crisis to a non-crisis status, the latter defined by a period of at least two consecutive years with inflation below 40 per cent.[17] He has suggested, however, that there is plenty of room to improve on this line of research.

Conclusions and Policy Implications

The literature on stabilisation has evolved substantially in the last four decades on the back of the knowledge gained from formal stabilisation episodes usually pursued under the guidance of the IMF. But the limited information on heterodox or non-IMF episodes has created a biased leaning against the analysis of orthodox plans both in terms of ERBS and MBS programmes.

The bias has limited the ability of countries to implement self-managed stabilisation policies, creating an apparent dependence on the IMF as a crisis manager and lender of last resort in situations of chronic inflation and balance of payments misalignments. This has raised a number of criticisms regarding the effectiveness and potential moral hazards of the IMF and other allied institutions.

Hopefully, the literature will continue to provide research and facts that could help countries avoid or minimize the occurrences of crisis and the dependence on institutions like the IMF in the design and implementation of stabilisation policies around the world. There is, however, a sizeable research gap that needs to be fulfilled. For example, policy-makers need to better understand the role of credibility in stabilizing, or even more important, in preventing macroeconomic misalignments. Is credibility enhanced by institutions like the IMF or by the type stabilisation strategy been pursued? Is there a relationship between the announcement and implementation of macroeconomic policy and the perceptions of agents on the success of stabilisation strategies that could have profound welfare effects? Is the timing of stabilisation plans relevant in minimizing or even so, in preventing crisis? Does the degree of capital mobility and currency substitution resulting from globalization affect the outcome of stabilisation polices? Do structural changes that are obviously present during times of severe volatility, affect the ability of government to measure and predict the impact of their stabilisation policies? The following chapters in this book aim at contributing to this knowledge and to answer some of these policy questions, helping to shape our understanding of stabilisation efforts in general and IMF-backed programmes in particular.

---

[17] The threshold definition of a crisis and non-crisis state based on a 40 per cent level of inflation and a delay of two years has been highly criticized, and is considered ambiguous or arbitrary (see Hamann 2001).

References

Agénor, P. R., and J. S. Bhandari, 1991, *Credibility, Expectations, and the Collapse of Stabilization Programs*, International Monetary Fund.

Agénor, P. R., and M. K., Taylor, 1992, Testing for Credibility Effects, *IMF Staff Papers*, 39 (3), 545-571.

Agénor, P. R., and P.J., Montiel, 1999, *Development Macroeconomics*, Princeton University Press.

Ahmad, S., 1986, Rural-Urban Migration–Policy Simulations in a Dual Economy Model of Bangladesh, *The Developing Economies*, 24 (1), 26-43.

Aisen, A., 1994, Money-Based Versus Exchange-Rate-Based Stabilisation: Is There Space for Political Opportunism?, *IMF Working Paper*, 4.

Alesina, A., and A. Drazen., 1991, Why are Stabilisations Delayed? *American Economic Review* 81 (5), 1170-1188.

Auernheimer, L., 1987, On the Outcome of Inconsistent Programs under Exchange Rate and Monetary Rules, *Journal of Monetary Economics*, 19, 279-305.

Ball, L., 1994, What Determines the Sacrifice Ratio? in N.G. Mankiw, (eds.) *Monetary Policy*, *NBER Working Papers*, 4306, National Bureau of Economic Research.

Barro, R. J., 1986, Reputation in a Model of Monetary Policy with Incomplete Information, *Journal of' Monetary Economics*, 17, 3-20.

Barro, R. J., and D. B. Gordon, 1983, A Positive Theory of Monetary Policy in a Natural-Rate Model, *Journal of Political Economy*, 91, 589-610.

Bird, G., 2002, The Credibility and Signaling Effect of IMF Programs, *Journal of Policy Modeling*, 24 (9), 799-811.

Blinder, A. S., and L. J. Maccini, 1991, Taking Stock: A Critical Assessment of Recent Research on Inventories, *Journal of Economic Perspectives*, 1991, 5 (1), 73-96.

Bordo, M. D., and A. Redish, 1990, Credible Commitment and Exchange Rate Stability: Canada's Interwar Experience, *Canadian Journal of Economics*, 23, 357-380.

Boyer, R. S., 1978, Optimal Foreign Exchange Market Intervention, *Journal of Political Economy*, 86 (6), 1045-1055.

Brainard, W., 1967, Uncertainty and the Effectiveness of Policy, *American Economic Review*, 57, 411-425.

Bruno, M., 1979, Stabilization and Stagflation in a Semi Industrialized Economy, in R. Dornbusch and J.A. Frenkel (eds.) *International Economic Policy*, Johns Hopkins University Press.

Bruno, M., S. Fisher, E. Helpman, N. Liviatan, and L. Meridor, 1990, *Lessons of Economic Stabilisation and its Aftermath*, MIT Press.

Cagan, P., 1956, The Monetary Dynamics of Hyperinflation, in Milton Friedman (eds.) *Study in the Quantity Theory of Money*, University of Chicago Press.

Calvo, G. A., 1983, Staggered Prices in a Utility Maximization Framework, *Journal of Monetary Economics*, 12, 383-398.

—. 1986, Temporary Stabilization: Predetermined Exchange Rates, *Journal of Political Economy*. 94, 1319-1329.

—. 2007, Interest Rate Rules, Inflation Stabilization, and Imperfect Credibility: The Small Open Economy Case, *NBER Working Papers*, 13177, National Bureau of Economic Research.

Calvo, G. A., and C. A., Végh, 1993, Exchange Rate-Based Stabilization Under Imperfect Credibility, in H. Frisco and A. Worgotter, (eds.) *Open-Economy Macroeconomics*, MacMillan, 3-28.

—. 1999, Inflation Stabilization and BOP Crises in Developing Countries, in Taylor, J.B. and M. Woodford, (eds.) *Handbook of Macroeconomics*, 1, 1531–1614.

—. 1994, Inflation Stabilization and Nominal Anchors, *Contemporary Economic Policy*, 12, 35-45.

Chadha, B., P. Masson, and G. Meredith, 1992, Models of Inflation and the Costs of Disinflation, *IMF Staff Papers*, 39, 395-431.

Cooper, R. N., 1971, Currency Devaluation in Developing Countries, in G. Ranis (eds.) *Government and Economic Development*, Yale University Press.

Cukierman, A., 1991, *Central Bank Behavior, Credibility, Accommodation and Stabilization*, MIT Press.

De Gregorio, J., P. E. Guidotti, and C. A. Végh, 1998, Inflation Stabilization and the Consumption of Durable Goods, *Economic Journal*, 108, 105-131.

Diaz-Alejandro, C.F., 1963, A Note on the Impact of Devaluation and Distributive Effect, *Journal of Political Economy*, 71 (2), 577-80.

Dornbusch, R., 1973, Devaluation, Money and Non-Traded Goods, *American Economic Review*, 63 (5), 871-80.

—. 1980, *Open Economy Macroeconomics*, Basic Books.

Dornbusch, R., and A. Werner, 1994, Mexico: Stabilization, Reform and No Growth, *Brookings Papers on Economic Activity*, 1, 253-315.

Dornbusch, R., and M. H. Simonsen, 1988, Inflation Stabilization: The Role of Incomes Policy and of Monetization, in Dornbusch, R., (eds) *Exchange Rates and Inflation*, MIT Press.

Dornbusch, R., and S. Fischer, 1986, Stopping Hyperinflation: Past and Present, *NBER Working Papers*, National Bureau of Economic Research, 1810.

Drazen, A, and V. Grilli, 1993, The Benefit of Crises for Economic Reforms. *American Economic Review*, 83 (3), 598-607.

Dreher, A., 2006, IMF Economic Growth: The Effects of Programs, Loans, and Compliance with Conditionality, *World Development*, 34 (5), 769-788.

Easterly, W., 1996, When is Stabilization Expansionary? Evidence from High Inflation, *Economic Policy*, 34.

Edwards, S., 1992, Exchange Rates as Nominal Anchors, *NBER Working Papers*, National Bureau of Economic Research, 4246.

—. 1996, Exchange Rate Anchors, Credibility and Inertia: A Tale of Two Crises: Chile and Mexico, *American Economic Review*, 86 (2), 176-180.

—. 1998, Two Crises: Inflationary Inertia and Credibility, *The Economic Journal*, 108, 665-80.

Erceg, C.J., and A.T. Levin, 1996, Structures Investment and the Dynamic Behaviour of the Real Exchange Rate, *Working Paper*, Board of Governors of the Federal Reserve System, Washington, DC.

Fernandez, R., and D. Rodrik, 1991, Resistance to Reform: Status Quo Bias in the Presence of Individual-Specific Uncertainty, *American Economic Review*, 81 (5) 1146-1155.

Fischer, S., 1977, Long-Term Contracts, Rational Expectations, and the Optimal Money Supply Rule, *Journal of Political Economy*, 85 (2), 191-205.

—. 1986, *Exchange Rate versus Money Targets in Disinflation, in: Indexing, Inflation and Economic Policy*, MIT Press, 247-262.

—. 1999, On the Need for an International Lender of Last Resort, *Journal of Economic Perspectives*, 13 (4), 85-104.

Fischer, S., R. Sahay, and C. A. Végh, 2002, Modern Hyper and High Inflations, *Journal of Economic Literature*, 40, 837-880.

Flood, R. P., 1983, Comment, in: J. A. Frenkel (eds.) *Exchange Rates and International Macroeconomics*, University of Chicago Press.

Flood, R., and N. Marion, 1994, The Size and Timing of Devaluations in Capital-Controlled Developing Countries, *NBER Working Papers*, National Bureau of Economic Research, 4957.

Friedman, M., 1953, The Case for Flexible Exchange Rates, in: *Essays in Positive Economics*, 153-203, University of Chicago Press.

—. 1968, The Role of Monetary Policy, *American Economic Review*, 58 (1), 1-17.

Funke, N., 1993, Timing and Sequencing of Reforms: Competing Views and the Role of Credibility, *Kyklos*, 46, 337-362.

Gil-Diaz, F., and A. Carstens, 1996, One Year of Solitude: Some Pilgrim Tales about Mexico's 1994-1995 Crisis, *American Economic Review*, 82 (2), 164-169.

Goldstein, M. 2000: IMF Structural Programs, In: Joyce, J. P. (ed.), Economic and Financial Crises in Emerging Market Economies, University of Chicago, Chicago, 363-437.

Gylfason, T., 1987, Credit Policy and Economic Activity in Developing Countries with IMF Stabilization Programs, *Princeton Studies in International Finance*, 60.

Hamman, J. A., 2001, Exchange-Rate-Based Stabilisation: A Critical Look at the Stylized Facts, *IMF Staff Papers*, 48 (1), 111-138.

Hiemenz, U., P. Nunnenkamp and J.P. Agarwal, 1992, The International Competitiveness of Developing Countries for Risk Capital, *Kieler Studien*, 242.

Holt, C. C., F. Modigliani, J. F. Muth, H. A. Simon, 1960, *Planning Production, Inventories, and Work Force*, Prentice Hall Inc., Englewood Cliffs.

Joyce, J.P., 2004, The Adoption, Implementation, and Impact of IMF Programmes: A Review of the Issues and Evidence, *Comparative Economic Studies*, 46 (3), 451-467.

Kamin, S. B., 2001, Real Exchange Rates and Inflation in Exchange-Rate-Based Stabilizations: An Empirical Examination, *Journal of Development Economics*, 64, 237-253.

Khan, M.S., and M. D., Knight, 1982, Some Theoretical and Empirical Issues Relating to Economic Stabilization in Developing Countries, *World Development,* 10 (9), 709-30.

Knot, K., and J. Sturm, and J. Haan, 1998, The Credibility of the European Exchange Rate Mechanism, *Oxford Economic Papers*, Oxford University Press.

Krugman, P., and L. Taylor, 1978, Contractionary Effects of Devaluation, *Journal of International Economics*, 8 (2), 445-56.

Laban, R., and F. Sturzenegger, 1994a, Distributional Conflict, Financial Adaptation and Delayed Stabilization, *Economics and Politics*, 6 (3), 257-276.

—. 1994b, Fiscal Conservatism as a Response to the Debt Crisis, *Journal of Development Economics*, 45 (2), 305-324.

Lahiri, A., 2000, Disinflation Programs under Policy Uncertainty, *Journal of International Economics*, 50, 351-373.

—. 2001. Exchange Rate Based Stabilization under Real Frictions, *Journal of Economic Dynamics and Control*, 25, 1157-77.

Lipton, D., and J. Sachs, 1990, Creating a Market Economy in Eastern Europe: The Case of Poland, *Brookings Papers on Economic Activity*, 1, 75-133.

Marchesi, S., 2003, Adoption of an IMF Program and Debt Rescheduling: An Empirical Analysis, *Journal of Development Economics*, 70 (2), 403-423.

Metzler, L. A., 1941, The Nature and Stability of Inventory Cycles, *Review of Economics and Statistics*, 23, 113-129.

Mondino, G., F. Sturzenegger, and M. Tommasi, 1996, Recurrent High Inflation and Stabilization: A Dynamic Game. *International Economic Review*, 37, (4) 981-996.

Mundell, R. A., 1963, Inflation and Real Interest, *Journal of Political Economy*, 71 (6), 280-283.

Murphy, K., A. Sheifler, and R. Vishny, 1992, The Transition to a Market Economy: Pitfalls of Partial Reform, *Quarterly Journal of Economics*, 107 (3), 889-906.

Mussa, M, 1984, The Adjustment Process and the Timing of Trade Liberalization, *NBER Working Paper Series*, National Bureau of Economic Research, 1458.

Mussa, M., and M., Savastano, 1999, The IMF Approach to Economic Stabilization, *NBER Macroeconomics Annual*, Cambridge, MA: MIT Press.

Nowzad, B., 1981, Debt in Developing Countries: Some Issues for the 1980's, *Finance and Development*, 19 (1), 13-16.

Nsouli, S. M., M. Rached, and N. Funke, 2002, The Speed of Adjustment and the Sequencing of Economic Reforms: Issues and Guidelines for Policymakers, *IMF Working Paper Series*, International Monetary Fund, 132.

Okun, A. M., 1962, Potential GNP: Its Measurement and Significance, In Proceedings of the Business and Economics Statistics Section, *American Statistical Association*, 98-103.

Pazos, F., 1972, *Chronic Inflation in Latin America*, Praeger Publishers.

Persson, T., and G., Tabellini, 1990, *Macroeconomic Policy, Credibility and Politics*, Harwood Academic Publishing.

Phillips, A. W. 1958. The Relationship between Unemployment and the Rate of Change of Money Wages in the United Kingdom, 1861-1957, *Economica*, 25 (November), 283-299.

Polack, R.J., 1957, Monetary Analysis of Income Formation and Payments Problems, *IMF Staff Papers*, 6 (1), 1-50.

Poole, W., 1970, Optimal Choice of Monetary Instruments in a Simple Stochastic Macro Model, *Quarterly Journal of Economics*, 84 (May), 197-216.

Prazmowski, P. A., 2002, Endogenous Credibility and Stabilisation Programmes: Evidence from the Dominican Republic, *Applied Economic Letters*, 9, 933-937.

Rebelo, S., and C. A., Végh, 1995, Real Effects of Exchange-Rate-Based Stabilization: An Analysis of Competing Theories, *NBER Macro Annual*.

Reinhart, C. M., and C. A., Végh, 1995, Nominal Interest Rates, Consumption Booms, and Lack of Credibility: A Quantitative Examination, *Journal of Development Economics*, 46, 357-378.

Rodriguez, C.A., 1982. The Argentine Stabilization Program of December 20th, *World Development*, 10, 801-811.

Rogoff, K., 1985, The Optimal Degree of Commitment to an Intermediate Monetary Target, *Quarterly Journal of Economics*, 100 (November), 1169-1189.

Roldos, J., 1995, Supply-Side Effects of Disinflation Programs, *IMF Staff Papers*, 42, 158-183.

Salter, W. E., 1959, Internal and External Balance: The Role of Prices and Expenditure Effects, *Economic Record*, 35, 226-38.

Sánchez-Fung, J. R., 2005, Exchange Rates, Monetary Policy and Interest Rates in the Dominican Republic during the 1990s Boom and New Millennium Crisis, *Journal of Latin American Studies*, 37 (4), 727-738.

Sargent, T. J., 1982, The Ends of Four Big Hyperinflations, in: R. E., Hall, (eds.) *Inflation: Causes and Consequences*, 41-97.

Sturzenegger, F., and M. Tommasi, 1998, *The Political Economy of Reform*, MIT Press.

Swan, T., 1960, Economic Control in a Dependent Economy, *Economic Record*, 36, 51-66.

Taylor, J. B., 1975, Monetary Policy during a Transition to Rational Expectations, *Journal of Political Economy*, 83 (December), 1009-1021.

—. 1979, Staggered Wage Setting in a Macro Model, *American Economic Review*, 69 (May), 108-113.

—. 1980, Aggregate Dynamics and Staggered Contracts, *Journal of Political Economy*, 88 (February), 1-23.

—. 1982, Establishing Credibility: A Rational Expectations Viewpoint, *American Economic Review*, 72 (May), 81-85.

Tinbergen, J., 1952, *On the Theory of Economic Policy*, North-Holland.

Tornell, A., and A. Velasco, 1998, Fiscal Discipline and the Choice of a Nominal Anchor in Stabilisation, *Journal of International Economics*, 46, 1-30.

Uribe, M., 1995, Exchange-Rate-Based Inflation Stabilization: The Initial Real Effects of Credible Plans, *International Finance Discussion Paper*, 503, Board of Governors of the Federal Reserve System, Washington, D.C.

Van Wijnbergen, S., 1983, Credit Policy, Inflation and Growth in a Financially Repressed Economy, *Journal of Development Economics*, 13 (1), 45-65.

—. 1986, Exchange Rate Management and Stabilization Policy in Developing Countries, *Journal of Development Economics*, 23 (2), 227-247.

Veiga, F.J., 2002, IMF Arrangements, Politics, and the Timing of Stabilisations, *NIPE Working Papers*, Nucleo de Investigacao em Politicas Economicas, Universidade do Minho.

Walsh, C. E., 1995, Optimal Contracts for Central Bankers, *American Economic Review*, 85 (3), 150-167.

Williamson, J., 1981, *Exchange Rate Rules: The Theory, Performance and Prospects of the Crawling Peg*, St. Martin's Pre

CHAPTER THREE

THE STOCHASTIC LIFE CYCLE PERMANENT INCOME MODEL DURING STABILISATION

Introduction

Consumption is characterized by drop-recovery patterns during episodes of stabilisation. The stylized facts show that during *exchange-rate-based stabilisation* (ERBS) consumption begins with a boom and end with a slowdown, whereas under *money-based stabilisation* (MBS) programmes, consumption initially drops and later recovers (see, for example, Végh 1989; Kiguel and Liviatan 1992).

Within the literature on ERBS, there are four leading explanations classified as demand-side and supply-side approaches. In the former, the *temporariness hypothesis* pioneered by Calvo (1986), and later extended by Calvo and Végh (1999), rests on the notion that agents perceive the stabilisation programme to be temporary. As a consequence, consumer expenditure will increase while conditions remain stable and subsequently contract as expectations concerning the failure of the programme materialize.

The second explanation holds that stabilisation policies create wealth and income effects that bring forward unplanned consumption, creating an early boom followed by a later contraction (see, for example, De Gregorio et al 1998). The third explanation is based on backward-looking inflation expectations which was originated by Rodriguez (1982) following Cagan (1956). According to Rodriguez (1982), consumption is linked to interest rates and exchange rates. If *uncovered interest parity* (UIP) holds, interest rates fall proportionally with the exchange rate as a result of stabilisation policies. The fall in interest rates causes an increase in consumption followed by a later drop as conditions stabilize. Finally, the supply-side argues that inflation is a tax that, when controlled or reduced by the stabilisation programme, will modify consumers' preferences creating an initial boom followed by a contraction (see Lahiri 2001; Rebelo and Vègh 1995).

This chapter explores an alternative demand-side explanation that accounts for the patterns observed in consumption during both ERBS and MBS programmes. The modelling extends Hall's (1978) *stochastic life cycle-permanent income* (SLCPI) model allowing for capital mobility and currency substitution in the allocation of savings.

According to the *currency substitution-capital mobility* literature for developing countries, financial system inefficiencies, such as non-competitive financial markets and portfolio shifts between domestic and foreign money, will cause international financial variables to influence domestic portfolio allocation decisions (see Arango and Nadiri 1981).

The model shows that consumption expenditure is affected by foreign real interest rates, domestic interest rates and the exchange rate. It also illustrates that the performance of these variables during stabilisation can create wealth and income effects that capture the business cycle associated with consumption during and after the programmes' introduction. The chapter applies the model to the Argentine, Brazilian and Mexican ERBS programmes of 1991, 1994 and 1987, and to the Peruvian and Dominican Republic (DR) MBS programmes of 1990 and 1991.

Two important contributions can be highlighted. Firstly, by incorporating these extensions the SLCPI model is better suited to understanding consumption in the developing world. Developing countries are characterized by significant volatility, where exchange rates and international interest rates play a leading role in the formation of expectations.

Secondly, it allows understanding the consumption patterns observed during episodes of stabilisation that are closely related to the way central banks deal with the exchange rate and interest rates in controlling inflation. If these extensions have an empirical relevance, both governments and the *International Monetary Fund* (IMF) could benefit from being able to measure the impact of stabilisation while improving the designs of their packages.

Section 3.2 develops an extension of the SLCPI with a rational expectations model to account for currency substitution and capital mobility. Section 3.3 runs the econometric exercise for the selected countries. Section 3.4 evaluates the performance of the model during stabilisation in general and during ERBS and MBS in particular. Section 3.5 concludes.

Extending the SLCPI Model

In a very influential paper, Hall (1978) showed that under rational expectations, the SLCPI model would predict that consumption expenditure would follow a random walk with drift. This implied that past values of income and consumption should not have any predictive power over future levels of consumer expenditure.

Although empirical research has yet to confirm this hypothesis, there is evidence that stock market prices have a significant forecasting role (Bilson 1980). One explanation is that agents in the stock market are better informed about the future of the economy than consumers. Another explanation is that Hall's findings are based on the invalid assumption that real interest rates are constant. Subsequent research has relaxed some assumptions of the original model, allowing ways to reconcile the existence of other explanatory variables within Hall's framework.

This paper extends the SLCPI model by incorporating foreign real interest rates and exchange rates. The extension should be relevant in countries subject to exchange rate volatility that react to information about the future of the economy (Dornbusch 1973).[1]

In doing so, the first step incorporates currency substitution and capital mobility by assuming that consumers place a fraction $0 \leq \phi < 1$ of their savings into foreign currency at a international interest rate $R_t^* = 1 + r_t^*$ and trace its performance, in local currency, by using the changes in the nominal exchange rate $S_t = 1 + s_t$.[2]

Under these assumptions, the intertemporal budget constraint of the representative agent is given by:

$$A_{t+i} \leq RA_{t+i-1} + R_{t+i}^* S_{t+i} \left(Y_{t+i-1} - C_{t+i-1}\right)\varphi + \left(Y_{t+i-1} - C_{t+i-1}\right)\left(1 - \varphi\right) \qquad (3.1)$$

---

[1] The model also incorporates the local real interest rate. However, for simplicity and without loss of generality, it has been assumed constant. This assumption may not be implausible provided that many developing countries are characterized by underdeveloped banking systems that lack competitive market clearing interest rates.

[2] In this setting, the allocation of savings into foreign currency is done at a given fraction φ. This implies that when agents determine their optimal consumption expenditure, they will account for the international environment. The resulting Euler equation from the optimization problem in this chapter is valid whether or not the consumer is constrained when allocating savings into foreign assets However, if φ is allowed to be chosen freely, the consumer optimization problems would have a pair of Euler equations describing the evolution of changes in consumption and changes in the allocation of savings into foreign money.

where A_t are total assets in domestic currency at the end of period t, Y_t is real per-capita disposable income in period t, C_t is real per-capita private consumption in period t, and $R=(1+r)$ is a constant local real interest rate. In addition, the *tranversality* condition is given by:

$$A_T \geq 0 \tag{3.2}$$

The consumer problem, with known death date *T*, is given by:

$$Max_{\{C_{t+i}\}} E_t\left[\sum_{i=0}^{T} \delta^i U(C_{t+i})\right] \tag{3.3}$$

where E_t is an expectations operator in period t, γ measures the relative risk aversion of consumers and $U(C_{t+i})$ is a well behaved utility function.

The maximization problem is carried on (3.3) subject to equations (3.1) and (3.2), producing the following *Lagrangean*:

$$\begin{aligned} L = E_t\Big\{ & \sum_{i=0}^{T} \delta^i U(C_{t+i}) - \sum_{i=0}^{T} \lambda_{t+i}\big[A_{t+i} - RA_{t+i-1} - R^*_{t+i} S_{t+i}(Y_{t+i-1} - C_{t+i-1})\varphi \\ & -(Y_{t+i-1} - C_{t+i-1})(1-\varphi)\big] + \lambda_T A_T \Big\} \end{aligned} \tag{3.4}$$

The first order conditions are:

$$\partial L/\partial C_{t+i} = E_t\left[\delta^i U'(C_{t+i}) - \lambda_{t+i+1} R^*_{t+i+1} S_{t+i+1}\varphi - \lambda_{t+i}(1-\varphi)\right] = 0 \tag{3.5}$$

$$\partial L/\partial A_{t+i} = E_t\left[\lambda_{t+i+1} R - \lambda_{t+i}\right] = 0 \tag{3.6}$$

$$\partial L/\partial A_T = E_t \lambda_T = 0 \tag{3.7}$$

Substituting (3.6) into (3.5) results in:

$$E_t\left[\delta^i U'(C_{t+i}) - \lambda_{t+i} R^*_{t+i+1} S_{t+i+1}\varphi/R - \lambda_{t+i}(1-\varphi)\right] = 0 \tag{3.8}$$

After manipulation, (3.8) becomes:

$$\delta^i E_t U'(C_{t+i}) = E_t \lambda_{t+i} X_{t+i+1} \tag{3.9}$$

where $X_{t+i+1} = R^*_{t+i+1} S_{t+i+1} \varphi / R + 1 - \varphi$ follows a *Martingale*.

From (3.9) and (3.6), the *Euler* equation for the consumer problem is given by:

$$E_t \left[U'(C_{t+i+1}) / U'(C_{t+i}) \right] = E_t \left[X_{t+i+1} / \delta^i R X_{t+i} \right] \tag{3.10}$$

Preferences are assumed *isoelastic* as in Hansen and Singleton (1983) such that:

$$U(C_{t+i}) = C^{\gamma}_{t+i} / \gamma \tag{3.11}$$

where $0 < \gamma \leq 1$. It is also assumed that any random variable Z_{t+i} follows a covariance stationary *Gaussian* process that is normally distributed with mean zero and variance σ^2 such that under rational expectations: $E_t \ln Z_{t+1} = \ln Z_{t+1} + \varepsilon^Z_{t+1}$, and where ε^Z_{t+1} is white noise. Using these assumptions, consumption expenditure between periods t and $t+1$ is given by:

$$\Delta \ln C_{t+1} = \alpha + \left[1/(\gamma - 1) \right] \Delta \ln X_{t+1} + \varepsilon_{t+1} \tag{3.12}$$

where $\alpha = \left(-\ln R - \ln \delta + \sigma^2/2 \right) / (\gamma - 1)$ and $\varepsilon_t = \varepsilon^C_t + \varepsilon^X_t$.

Taking a first order *Taylor* approximation:

$$\Delta \ln X_{t+1} \cong \left[\varphi / (1 - \varphi) \right] \Delta x_{t+1} \tag{3.13}$$

where $x_{t+1} = R^*_{t+1} S_{t+1} / R$, is a relative version of the *uncovered interest parity* (UIP) condition.

Using (3.13), equation (3.12) becomes:

$$\Delta c_{t+1} = \alpha + \beta \Delta x_{t+1} + \varepsilon_{t+1} \tag{3.14}$$

where $c_t = \ln C_t$, Δ is a difference operator, and ε_t represents "news" that are *orthogonal* to the information set.

In equation (3.14), $\beta = \varphi/(1-\varphi)(\gamma-1) < 0$ such that an expected increase (fall) in x_t will lower (rise) consumption transferring the fraction φ of the consumer savings into foreign (local) currency. Note that consumers will take advantage of the expected wealth-income effect created by an increase (decrease) in the relative rate of return x_t.

The impact of currency substitution and capital mobility over consumption will depend on both the degree of international exposure of the country (φ) as well as on the relative risk aversion of consumers (γ). A higher degree of international exposure will increase the sensitivity of the exchange rate and the interest rates over consumption. Higher values of relative risk aversion will reduce this sensitivity provided that consumers will be more reluctant to speculate against expected movements in x_t.

In addition to the above extensions, the model incorporates the changes in income, accounting for the possibility of credit constraints agents. In the spirit of Flavin (1981) and Campbell and Mankiw (1991), a percentage n of the population is assumed to be excessively sensitive to income changes.

Accordingly, equation (3.14) becomes:

$$\Delta c_{t+1} = a + b\Delta x_{t+1} + n\Delta y_{t+1} + v_{t+1} \qquad (3.15)$$

where $a = \alpha(1-n)$ and $b = \beta(1-n)$. The error term $v_t = n\varepsilon_t^Y + (1-n)\varepsilon_t$ is no longer *orthogonal* provided that "news" and income are likely to be correlated.

Equation (3.15) covers previous models found in the literature. If ϕ is set to zero, the results of Flavin (1981) and Campbell and Mankiw (1991) are obtained. If both ϕ and n are set to zero, equation (3.15) collapses to Hall's (1978) *random walk* model with drift. Bean (1986) also shows that specifications like (3.15) are compatible with error correction models found in the more recent econometric literature (see Banerjee et al 1993).

Testing the Empirical Relevance of the Model

This section estimates equation (3.15) for Argentina, Brazil, DR, Mexico, and Peru. The specification to be tested is given by:

$$\Delta c_{t+1} = a + b\Delta x_{t+1} + n\Delta y_{t+1} + v_{t+1} \tag{3.16}$$

where a can take any value, b should be strictly negative and n should fall between zero and unity. Equation (3.16) was estimated with annual data ranging from 1950 up to 2000, using real per capita private consumption (C_t), real per capita disposable income (Y_t) and a variable representing the relative return rate between local and foreign currencies (x_t).

The relative return was constructed for each country using the foreign real interest rate approximated by the real US Treasury Bills (R_t^*), and the log changes in the nominal exchange rate for each country with respect to the US (S_t).[3] Real variables are constructed using each county's consumer price index (P_t) and the US consumer price index. Table 3.1 summarizes the data, sources and definition.

Figures 3.1a-3.1e also provide a graphical representation of the data. The graphs illustrate that there exists a clear *stationarity* pattern between the log changes in real consumption expenditure, the log changes in real disposable income and the changes in x_t.

A very interesting feature is that the relationship between these variables intensifies during times of crisis. For example, in the DR and Peru, the pattern becomes more evident after the second half of the 1980s which was a period of high volatility characterized by several stabilisation episodes with IMF intervention.

This correlation is also present after 1970 in Mexico, when the exchange market was liberalised leading to a sequence of exchange rate crises followed by several stabilisation attempts. The same can be deduced from Argentina and Brazil's historical profiles.

This chapter will show that the model and its extensions provide a solid framework for studying consumption expenditure during times of significant exchange rate volatility that may accentuate the welfare implications of stabilisation policies in countries suffering from economic

[3]Alternatively, the yields on five and ten year medium and long-term US government bonds were also tested. The results favoured the specification using T-Bills.

crisis. One final aspect of the graphs is the strong correlation between changes in income and consumption.

Table 3.1: Data, range, sources and definitions

Variable		Definition	Range
Argentina			
	Ct	Domestic consumption of goods and services in real per capita terms. Deflated by GDP deflator (1990=100)	1960-2000
	Y_t	Gross Domestic Product in real per capita terms. Deflated by GDP deflator (1990=100)	1960-2000
	P_t	Average consumer price index (1990=100)	1960-2000
	ER_t	Average nominal "spot" exchange rate with respect to the US (Banking rate)	1960-2000
	X_t	[1+dlog(R*$_t$)-dlog(P*$_t$)*[1+dlog(ER$_t$)]	1960-2000
Brasil			
	Ct	Domestic consumption of goods and services in real per capita terms. Deflated by GDP deflator (1990=100)	1980-2000
	Y_t	Gross Domestic Product in real per capita terms. Deflated by GDP deflator (1990=100)	1980-2001
	P_t	Average consumer price index (1990=100)	1980-2002
	ER_t	Average nominal "spot" exchange rate with respect to the US (Banking rate)	1980-2003
	X_t	[1+dlog(R*$_t$)-dlog(P*$_t$)*[1+dlog(ER$_t$)]	1980-2004
DR			
	Ct	Domestic consumption of goods and services in real per capita terms. Deflated by GDP deflator (1990=100)	1950-2000
	Y_t	Gross Domestic Product in real per capita terms. Deflated by GDP deflator (1990=100)	1950-2000
	P_t	Average consumer price index (1990=100)	1950-2000
	ER_t	Average nominal "spot" exchange rate with respect to the US (Parallel market rate)	1950-2000
	X_t	[1+dlog(R*$_t$)-dlog(P*$_t$)*[1+dlog(ER$_t$)]	1950-2000
Mexico			
	Ct	Domestic consumption of goods and services in real per capita terms. Deflated by GDP deflator (1990=100)	1950-2000
	Y_t	Gross Domestic Product in real per capita terms. Deflated by GDP deflator (1990=100)	1950-2000
	P_t	Average consumer price index (1990=100)	1950-2000
	ER_t	Average nominal "spot" exchange rate with respect to the US (Banking rate)	1950-2000
	X_t	[1+dlog(R*$_t$)-dlog(P*$_t$)*[1+dlog(ER$_t$)]	1950-2000
Peru			
	Ct	Domestic consumption of goods and services in real per capita terms. Deflated by GDP deflator (1990=100)	1950-2000
	Y_t	Gross Domestic Product in real per capita terms. Deflated by GDP deflator (1990=100)	1950-2000
	P_t	Average consumer price index (1990=100)	1950-2000
	ER_t	Average nominal "spot" exchange rate with respect to the US (Banking rate)	1950-2000
	X_t	[1+dlog(R*$_t$)-dlog(P*$_t$)*[1+dlog(ER$_t$)]	1950-2000
US			
	R^*t	Real US Tresury Bill (3 moth averages)	1950-2000
	P^*_t	Average US Consumer price index (1990=100)	1950-2000

Soure: IMF International Financial Statistics.

This is a clear indication of the sensitivity of consumption to changes in income, understood in the literature, as credit constrained consumers. This is expected in developing countries that are characterized by income inequalities, significantly underdeveloped financial systems and limited access to international capital markets.

Figures 3.1a: Changes in consumption, income and x_t (Argentine)

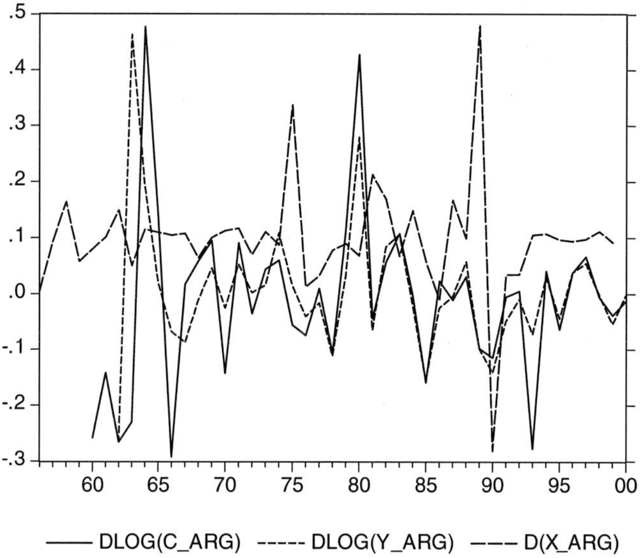

Figures 3.1b: Changes in consumption, income and x_t (Brazil)

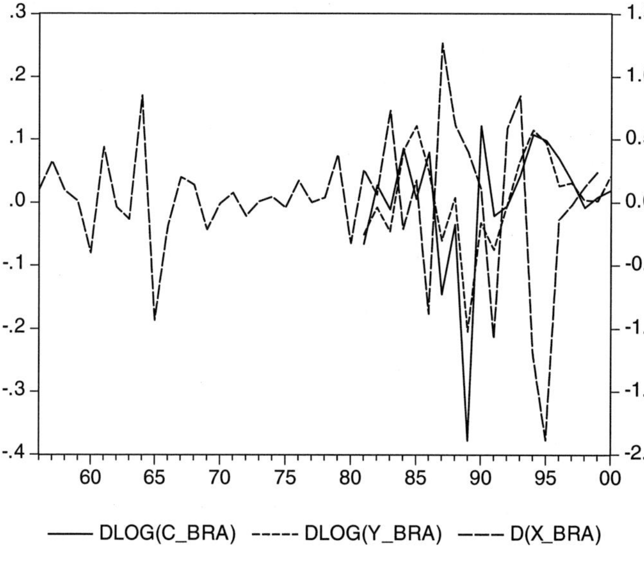

Figures 3.1c: Changes in consumption, income and x_t (DR)

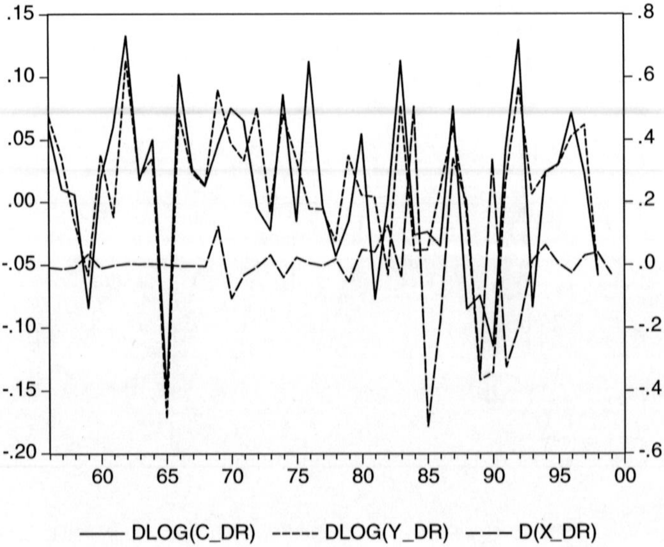

Figures 3.1d: Changes in consumption, income and x_t (Mexico)

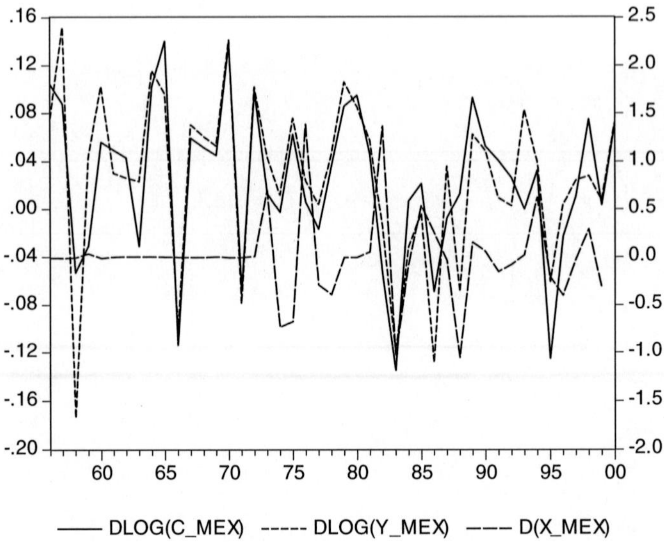

Figures 3.1e: Changes in consumption, income and x_t (Peru)

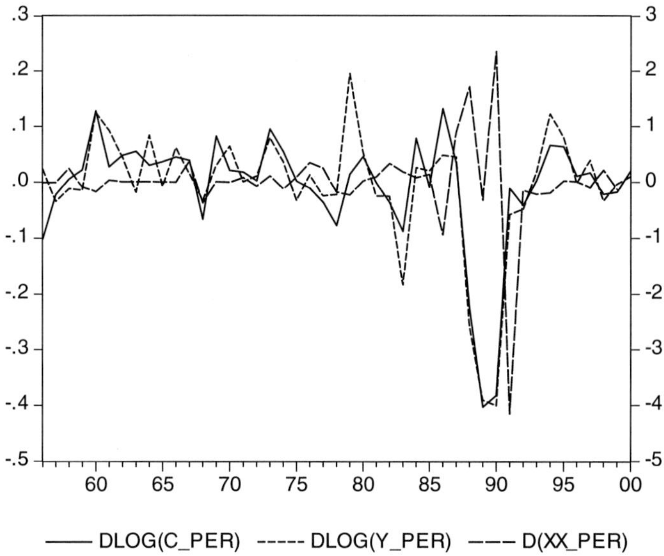

Beyond the graphical representation of the data, Table 3.2 shows the stationarity of the individual series using the ADF test (Dickey and Fuller, 1979). The results indicate that for all of the countries in the sample, the log of real per capita private consumption (c_t), the log of real per capita disposable income (y_t) and x_t follow $I(1)$ processes. This provides a consistent set of first differences covariance stationary processes compatible with the specification of equation (3.16).

Turning to the econometric exercise, Table 3.3 presents the estimation of equation (3.16) for each country. A *Generalized Method of Moments* (GMM) is employed since the residuals are likely to be correlated with income in violation of the *orthogonality* condition required for *Ordinary Least Squares* (OLS) estimation.[4]

[4] Several instruments were tested. In particular, lagged changes in consumption and income, as well as lagged values of x_t were used. As expected, changes in income have no predictive power over future consumption, whereas changes in consumption and relative interest rates have a significant effect. Over-identifying restrictions on the instruments using the J-statistic (see Newey and West 1987) were also tested, yielding values of χ_2^2 and χ_4^2 in the range of 1.83 and 2.49 for model (A) and of 1.73 and 2.30 for model (B).

Table 3.2: ADF test of stationarity for selected countries

Variables	Argentine†	Brazil†	DR††	Mexico†	Peru ††
c_t	-2.28	-0.14	-0.77	-1.66	-0.66
y_t	-1.87	-0.47	-0.93	-1.81	-0.66
x_t	-0.15	-1.47	-0.30	-0.56	-1.47
Δc_t	-8.48*	-4.53**	-7.51*	-6.30*	-4.06**
Δy_t	-5.46*	-2.99**	-6.12*	-6.26*	-4.32**
Δx_t	-3.41**	-9.44*	-8.93*	-4.92*	-3.77**

Notes: *, ** and *** denote significance at the 1%, 5% and 10% level under MacKinnon (1996). For the ADF test, the intercept and constant were excluded. Lag length selection based on the Schuartz information criteria. † and †† denote ERBS and MBS respectively.

As a way of assessing the relevance of capital mobility and currency substitution in the model, the proposed specification is compared to competing frameworks. In particular, column (A) presents the specification of Campbell and Mankiw (1991) that includes changes in income:

$$\Delta c_{t+1} = a + n\Delta y_{t+1} + v_{t+1} \quad (3.17)$$

and column (B) presents equation (3.16) which includes the changes in x_t. As proposed by Bean (1986), both specifications should be evaluated and compared, in addition to the conventional criteria, using the regressions standard errors. The different criteria indicate that model (B) is favoured to model (A) in describing the data generating process.[5]

The most relevant aspect of model (B), however, is its strong support for the assumption concerning capital mobility and currency substitution. As expected, the coefficient on x_t is negative and highly significant in all countries. The values range from minus 2 per cent to minus 18 per cent, except for the Peruvian case in which it is below 1 per cent.[6]

---

[5] A stationarity ADF test on the residuals, for all countries and under different specifications, provides evidence of cointegration (see Engle and Granger 1987).

[6] The result for Peru could be smoothing out the strong devaluation of the exchange rate prior to the introduction of the IMF stabilisation programme in 1990. This result is also consistent with the fact that Peru became a highly dollarized economy during the 1990s.

Table 3.3: GMM estimates of consumption equations (3.16 and 3.17) for selected countries.

Δc_{t+1}		Argentina†		Brazil†		DR††		Mexico†		Peru ††	
Variable	Coefficient	A	B	A	B	A	B	A	B	A	B
Constant	*a*	0.016	0.001	0.011	-0.002	0.008	0.001	-0.018	0.010	-0.005	-0.002
		(0.008)	(0.006)	(0.005)	(0.008)	(0.006)	(0.003)	(0.007)	(0.005)	(0.004)	(0.003)
Δx_{t+1}	*b*		-0.0001		-0.001		-0.115		-0.032		-0.0004
			(0.000)		(0.000)		(0.044)		(0.012)		(0.000)
Δy_{t+1}	*n*	1.588	0.955	0.875	0.892	0.389	0.716	1.215	0.676	0.965	0.865
		(0.285)	(0.086)	(0.088)	(0.097)	(0.210)	(0.107)	(0.136)	(0.155)	(0.016)	(0.019)
N		23	31	19	18	47	47	48	48	48	48
R^2		0.760	0.731	0.574	0.611	0.415	0.510	0.374	0.525	0.772	0.795
σ		0.065	0.063	0.075	0.076	0.050	0.046	0.057	0.050	0.050	0.047
J-statistic		0.142	0.129	0.117	0.250	0.209	0.161	0.151	0.177	0.128	0.131
DW											
ADF											

Notes: *, ** and *** denote significance at the 1%, 5% and 10% respectively. The estimation uses a quadratic kernel, the Newey-West bandwidth for the lag selection and a prewhitening simultaneous weighting matrix and coefficient iteration. † and †† denote ERBS and MBS respectively.

Regarding credit-constrained consumers, the coefficient n indicates that more than three quarters of the population in the countries under analysis are excessively sensitive to changes in income. The results are consistent with Bean (1986) and Flavin (1981) for the US, and Muellbauer (1983) and Wickens and Molana (1984) for the UK. Argentina, Brazil and Peru appear to be the most sensitive with coefficients above 85 per cent, whereas Mexico and the DR have lower sensitivity with coefficients around 60 per cent.[7]

Preferences in favour of foreign asset holdings (φ) can also be calculated from the analysis. Assuming a degree of relative risk aversion (γ) of around minus two (-2), which is reasonable for countries with a high risk profile as suggested by Bean (1986), indicate that preferences in favour of foreign asset holdings are around 54 per cent for Argentina, 77 per cent for Brazil, 61 per cent for the DR, 23 per cent for Mexico, and not more that 10 per cent in the Peruvian case. The result for Peru is consistent with the dollarization process that started in the 1990s, attenuating the sensitivity to changes in the exchange rate.

Model Performance during Stabilisation

The data suggests that most of the consumption patterns in the sample obey the stylized facts as implied by the type of anchor used during stabilisation. Figures 3.2a to 3.2e illustrate the evolution of real per capita consumption alongside changes in x_t.[8] The Mexican 1988 and Brazilian 1994 ERBS show consumption boom-drop cycles, and the Peruvian 1990 MBS has a drop-recovery pattern. On the contrary, the Argentine 1991 Convertibility ERBS plan shows a drop-recovery pattern while the DR MBS of 1991 shows a boom-drop sequence in contrast to the documented facts. It appears that the patterns suggested by the *recession-now-versus-recession-later* hypothesis are not unique when it comes to the type of nominal anchor used during stabilisation.

---

[7] The proximity of Mexico and the DR to the US, may contribute to this relatively low-income sensitivity, which also implies that aggregate consumption decisions are more weighted in favour of currency substitution and capital mobility.

[8] Note that figures 3.2a to 3.2e give a comparative representation of the relationship between consumption and x_t implied by the model. The graphical approach does not control, however, for other variables such as changes in income. Nevertheless, x_t provides a good description of consumption during stabilisation. The year of stabilisation is normalized to date *T*. The graph is dual scale, such that log consumption changes are in LHS and changes in x_t are in the RHS.

In the first group, Mexico and Brazil show an average increase in consumption of about 3 per cent at the time the stabilisation programme was introduced with a slowdown about two years after. For the Peruvian case, consumption felt by about 6 per cent in the first three years of the programme, with a recovery of 1.4 per cent in the fourth year after launching the programme. In the second group, Argentina shows a drop of 12 per cent with a recovery of 1.7 per cent one year after and a later fall of 2.7 per cent in the third year after the programme was introduced. The DR case shows an average consumption growth of 3.7 per cent during the first two years of the stabilisation episode and a later drop of 4 per cent in the third year after the programme was launched.[9]

The proposed model suggests that the drop-recovery sequence depends on several factors, that when combined, replicate the observed behaviour of consumption during stabilisation. Firstly, consumption will depend on the behaviour of the exchange rate and the foreign interest rate during stabilisation. Accordingly, the pattern of consumption will depend on the specific anchor used for stabilisation and its effects over x_t.

If, for example, MBS causes an increase in real interest rates due to a restrictive monetary policy and consequently the contraction in the monetary base stops the devaluation of the exchange rate, consumption will boom provided that agents will convert part of their total foreign assets into local currency in order to increase both local consumption and savings. If, however, real interest rates increase, but the widening of the interest rate gap raises devaluation expectations as in Sanchez-Fung and Prazmowski (2004), consumption will drop and savings in foreign assets will increase.

The same rationale holds for ERBS programmes. If ERBS is more effective in controlling inflation than MBS (i.e. provides a more credible anchor), consumption is more likely to perform in a boom-drop cycle. If, however, the anchor is not credible as in Calvo and Vègh (1999) and Calvo (1986), consumption will most likely show a drop-recovery pattern. In general, a reduction (increase) in x_t will cause consumption to drop (boom) when the expected movements in the exchange rate and real return rates create income and wealth effects.

On the other hand, the sensitivity of consumption to changes in x_t will depend on the degree of capital mobility, currency substitutions and relative risk aversion in the economy. The patterns observed in consumption will also depend on how the nominal anchor affects the degree of capital mobility and currency substitution during stabilisation.

---

[9] This pattern is consistent with the notion that there is a credibility effect by which the exchange rate appreciates and consumption recovers as raw materials and tradable goods become cheaper.

Figure 3.2a: Δc_t and Δx_t during selected stabilisation dates (Argentina)

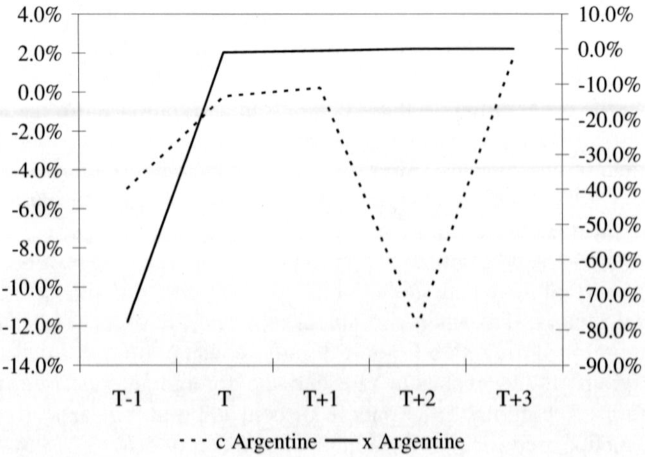

Figure 3.2b: Δc_t and Δx_t during selected stabilisation dates (Brazil)

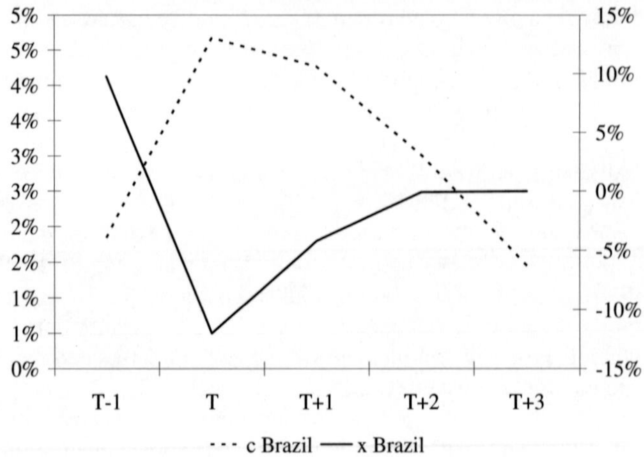

Figure 3.2c: Δc_t and Δx_t during selected stabilisation dates (DR)

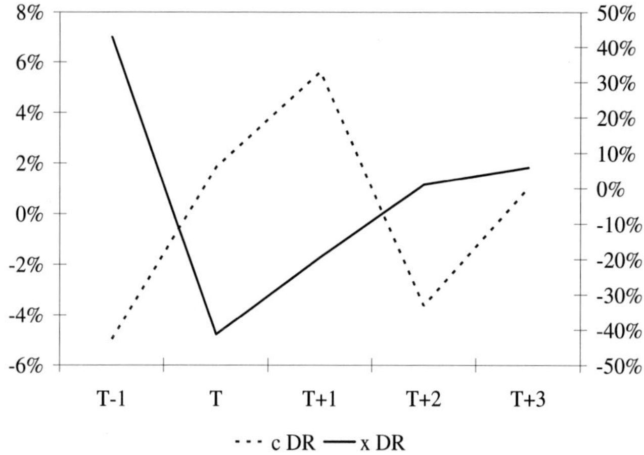

Figure 3.2d: Δc_t and Δx_t during selected stabilisation dates (Mexico)

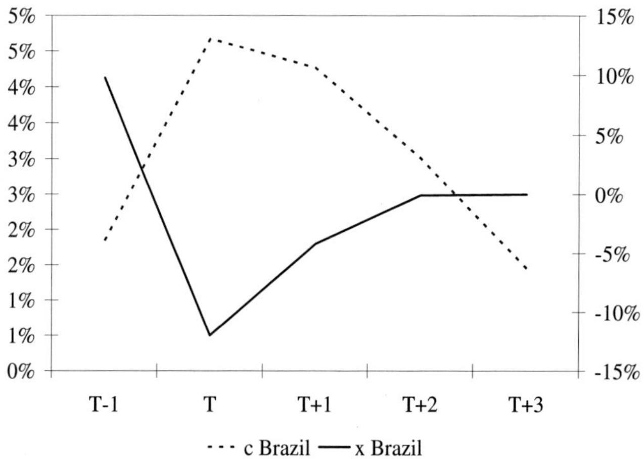

Figure 3.2e: Δc_t and Δx_t during selected stabilisation dates (Peru)

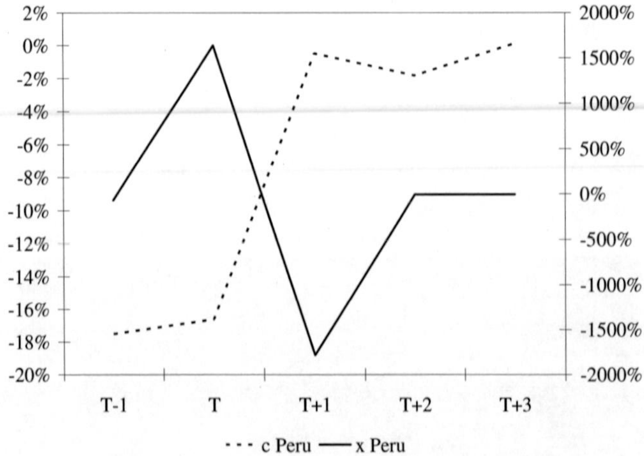

From the behaviour of Δc_t and Δx_t in Figures 3.2a-3.2e, it follows that equation (3.16) offers a good approximation of the stylized facts of stabilisation. It appears that a consistent negative relationship between these two variables exists even though some of the countries do not comply with the documented facts. This relationship is explained by both the theoretical and empirical findings.

Consequently, changes in x_t capture more than 70 per cent of the changes in consumption during stabilisation. The average absolute change in consumption implied by Δx_t is of about 2 per cent for the countries in the sample, whereas the actual observed change was of about 2.8 per cent. The remaining 0.8 per cent observed variation is explained by expected changes in income.

The extended version of the SLCPI model with rational expectations, currency substitution and capital mobility implies that when the exchange rate is expected to devalue (appreciate) or foreign interest rates are expected to increase (decrease), consumption expenditure will fall (rise) and savings in foreign assets will increase (decrease) as agents hedge against these expectations. Finally, consumption during episodes of stabilisation will depend on how exchange rates and interest rates react to the specific type nominal anchor used for stabilisation. In some cases, x_t falls and consequently consumption will rise, whereas in other circumstances x_t increases and consumption falls.

Conclusions and Policy Implications

This chapter finds that capital mobility and currency substitution are present in the consumption patterns of Argentina, Brazil, DR, Mexico, and Peru. The empirical analysis shows that local and foreign interest rates as well as the exchange rate play a role in consumers' portfolio allocations, as implied by the extended version of the *stochastic life cycle-permanent income* (SLCPI) with rational expectations model.

Regarding stabilisation programmes, the model provides an alternative demand side explanation for the consumption patterns observed in the stylized facts. In particular, capital mobility and currency substitution explain more than two thirds of the variations in consumption before and after stabilisation programmes are introduced. There is also evidence of a large share of consumers that are overly sensitive to anticipated changes in income. According to the literature, this sensitivity is due to credit limitations.

From a policy perspective, the findings indicate that a weakening of the local environment relative to the rest of the world could trigger significant capital flights. If agents perceive that the currency could devalue, consumption will drop in order to increase saving in foreign assets. Hence, exchange rates expectations may initiate significant capital flights that could lead to inflation and a recession. Therefore, the model cautions governments on the potential effects of negative expectations over social welfare.

The strong degree of income sensitivity found in the analysis also opens a critical door for the effectiveness of income polices. However, caution is needed if the share of consumers regarded as financially constrained is among the low-income group. In an effort to deceive devaluation expectations, restrictive monetary policy could have larger negative welfare implications as consumers that are credit constraint will receive the largest burden affecting both income and consumption. Finally, and during times of crisis, the way stabilisation packages affect the evolution of interest rates, exchange rates and inflation will have significant different effects over consumption that may not fall within the reported stylized facts and that should be taken into consideration when evaluating the effects of stabilisation packages.

References

Arango, S. and M. I. Nadiri, 1981, Demand for Money in Open Economies, *Journal of Monetary Economics*, 7, 69-83.

Banerjee, A., J. Dolado, J. W. Galbraith, and D. F. Hendry, 1993, *Co-integration, Error-Correction, and the Econometric Analysis of Non-Stationary Data*, Oxford University Press.

Bean, C. R., 1986, The Estimation of "Surprise" Models and the "Surprise" Consumption Function, *The Review of Economic Studies*, 53, 497-516.

Bilson, J. F., 1980, The Rational Expectations Approach to the Consumption Function: A Multi Country Study, *European Economic Review*, 13, 273-299.

Cagan, P., 1956, The Monetary Dynamics of Hyperinflation, in Friedman M., (eds.) *Studies in the Quantity Theory of Money*, University of Chicago Press, 25-117.

Calvo, G. A., 1986.,Temporary Stabilisation: Predetermined Exchange Rates, *Journal of Political Economy*, 94, 1319-29.

Calvo, G.A., and C.A. Végh, 1999, Inflation Stabilization and BOP Crises in Developing Countries, in J.B., Taylor and M. Woodford, (eds.). *Handbook of Macroeconomics*, 1, 1531–1614.

Campbell, J.Y., and N.G. Mankiw, 1991, The Response of Consumption to Income: A Cross-Country Investigation, *European Economic Review*, 35, 723-767.

De Gregorio, J., P. E. Guidotti, and C. A. Végh, 1998, Inflation Stabilization and Consumption of Durable Goods, *Economic Journal*, 108, 105-31.

Dickey, D. A., and W. A. Fuller, 1979, Distribution of the Estimators for Autoregressive Time Series with a Unit Root, *Journal of the American Statistical Association*, 74, 427-431.

Dornbusch, R., 1973, Devaluation, Money and Non-Traded Goods, *American Economic Review*, 63 (5), 871-80.

Engle, R. F. and C. W. J. Granger, 1987, Co-integration and Error Correction: Representation, Estimation, and Testing, *Econometrica*, 55, 251-276.

Flavin, M., 1981, The Adjustment of Consumption to Changing Expectations about Future Income, *Journal of Political Economy*, 89, 974-1009.

Hall, R. E., 1978, Stochastic Implications of the Life-Cycle Permanent Income Hypothesis: Theory and Evidence, *Journal of Political Economy*, 89, 971-987.

Hansen, L. P., and K. J. Singleton, 1983, Stochastic Consumption, Risk Aversion, and the Temporal Behavior of Asset Returns, *Journal of Political Economy*, 91, 249-265.

Kiguel, M., and N., Liviatan, 1992, The Business Cycle Associated with Exchange Rate-Based Stabilisations, *The World Bank Economic Review,* 6 (2), 279–305.

Lahiri, A., 2001, Exchange Rate Based Stabilisation under Real Frictions, *Journal of Economic Dynamics and Control*, 25, 1157-77.

MacKinnon, J.G., 1991, Critical Values for Cointegration Tests, Chapter 13 in R.F. Engle and C. W. J. Granger, (eds.), *Long-run Economic Relationships: Readings in Cointegration*, Oxford University Press.

—. 1996, Numerical Distribution Functions for Unit Root and Cointegration Tests, *Journal of Applied Econometrics*, 11, 601-618.

Muellbauer, J., 1983, Surprises in the Consumption Function, *Economic Journal*, 93, 34-50.

Newey, Whitney and K. West, 1987, Hypothesis Testing with Efficient Method of Moments Estimation, *International Economic Review*, 28, 777-787.

Rebelo, S. and C. A. Végh., 1995, Real Effects of Exchange Rate Based Stabilization: An Analysis of Competing Theories, *NBER Macroeconomics Annual*, 125-74.

Rodriguez, C. A., 1982, The Argentine Stabilization Plan of December 20th, *World Development*, 10, 801-11.

Sánchez–Fung, J. R., and P. A. Prazmowski, 2004, PPP, Random Walks, and UIP after Interest Rate Liberalization in a Small Developing Economy, *Economics Bulletin*, 6 (1), 1–7.

Végh, C. A., 1989, Stopping High Inflation: An Analytical Overview, *IMF Staff Papers*, 39, 629-95.

Wickens, M.R., and H. Molana, 1984, Stochastic Life Cycle Theory with Rational Expectations, *Review of Economic Studies*, 49, 55-67.

Young, P., D. Dunn, A. Giustiniani, F. N. De-Simone, E. Tanner, and J. McHugh, 1999, Dominican Republic: selected issues, *IMF Staff Report*, (October), 99-117, International Monetary Fund.

CHAPTER FOUR

CREDIBILITY, INFLATION AND REAL EXCHANGE RATES DURING STABILISATION

Introduction

Real exchange rates tend to appreciate after *exchange rate-based stabilisation* (ERBS) programmes are introduced. The real appreciation of the currency can create large and unsustainable current account deficits, aggravating the outcome of countries suffering from chronic inflation. This stylized fact, which is well documented in the literature, has produced three plausible explanations that focus on the reason why domestic inflation continues after an ERBS programme is introduced (see, for instance, Calvo and Végh 1999; Fischer et al 2002).

The first explanation argues that some stabilisation policies boost aggregate demand causing inflation in non-tradable prices (see, for example, Calvo and Végh 1993; Rebelo and Végh 1994; Erceg and Levin 1996). The second explanation states that inflation converges slowly to international levels due to overlapping contracts and backward-looking expectations (see Rodríguez 1982; Dornbusch and Werner 1994; Edwards 1992). The final and more recent explanation argues that domestic inflation reacts to the gap between the real exchange rate and its equilibrium level.

If balance of payments misalignments and a devalued currency cause the real exchange rate to be away from its equilibrium prior to stabilisation, non-tradable inflation will continue until equilibrium is restored (see Kamin 2001; Gil-Diaz and Carstens 1996). Consequently, under a nominal exchange rate anchor, implied by the stabilisation programme, the sustained increase in domestic prices advanced by these three explanations, will lead to an appreciation of the real exchange rate.

There have been several approaches in testing the empirical relevance of the above hypotheses. For example, Kamin (2001) used a model that decomposes the real appreciation of the exchange rate into the parts attributed to departures from equilibrium, the growth of domestic demand,

and the one coming from inflation inertia. Using data for Mexico, Kamin (2001) shows that inflation reacts to all three explanations but that their relative relevance change over time. A recursive coefficient approach, however, finds that the estimated inflation equations lack parameter stability particularly around the time of stabilisation episodes. Unfortunately, the analysis cannot determine if the lack of stability is due to a poorly specified model or to Lucas (1976) deep structural parameters changes.

Interestingly, Edwards (1998) has shown that inflation may be difficult to control if there is a low degree of credibility on the stabilisation attempt. Using two distinctive stabilisation episodes in Chile and Mexico, he finds that changes in credibility are reflected in the coefficients of estimated inflation equations.

This chapter extends Kamin's (2001) approach by incorporating the concept of credibility advanced in Edwards (1998). In particular, the model accounts for the time-varying parameters found in the estimation of inflation equations during the implementation of stabilisation plans. The analysis shows that credibility is central in determining how inflation reacts to departures from equilibrium, to changes in output and to inertia.

According to the model, a credible ERBS programme will eliminate inertia causing an immediate convergence of inflation to international levels. A less than fully credible programme, however, will cause a significant degree of persistence, a slow decline of inflation to international levels, and a substantial appreciation of the real exchange rate. The model is tested on Chile's 1977 and Mexico's 1998 and 1995 ERBS programmes.

This exercise delivers some important contributions: Firstly, it shows that changes in credibility can produce significant parameter instability in the estimation of structural equations especially during times of significant macroeconomic volatility. Secondly, for Chile and Mexico, it concludes that credibility depends on the flexibility allowed to the nominal anchor during the implementation of the programmes and not on the way wages are set. Thirdly, recursive time-varying coefficients can provide relevant information about the performance of the stabilisation programme and should be the preferred modelling strategy when dealing with episodes of chronic inflation. Finally, if these parameters changes are ignored, the empirical assessment carried out by central banks and the *International Monetary Fund* (IMF) could be misleading in the design and management of exchange rate policies in general and during the implementation of stabilisation plans in particular.[1]

[1] The concept of parameter instability and its relationship with poor out-of-sample performance of exchange rate models, especially when compared to forecast of the random walk, was first highlighted by Meese and Rogoff (1983).

Section 4.2 highlights Chile's and Mexico's reforms. Section 4.3 develops the theoretical framework. Section 4.4 presents the data, runs the econometric models, and discusses the empirical results. Section 4.5 concludes.

Stabilisation and Structural Reforms in Chile and Mexico

Before proceeding with the formal modelling strategy and econometric exercise, it is important to highlight and compare some of the salient features of Chile's 1978 programme with those of the Mexican 1988 and 1995 plans. Chile and Mexico have been chosen as references, given their relevance to many of the subsequent stabilisation episodes that could have benefitted by looking back at their performance.

Chile and Mexico reforms share a number of common features including an opening of the economy, deregulation and privatization of state-owned companies, and a stabilisation programme based on the exchange rate as the nominal anchor. They also had important differences. In Chile, the formal programme started in 1978 and had two stages: beginning in February 1978 up to June 1979, the rate of devaluation was preannounced and set below the inflation rate under parity. After June 1979, the nominal exchange rate was pegged at 39 pesos per US dollar.

A fundamental aspect of Chile's programme, one that has attracted considerable attention, was the way in which wages were set. Starting in 1978, the authorities adopted a formal backward looking mechanism in which wages were adjusted to compensate for past inflation.

Another important aspect of the programme was monetary policy. Prior to the introduction of the 1978 programme, money supply was relaxed and accommodative to the *crawling peg* regime that was followed by the central bank. Beginning in 1978, monetary policy was restrictive and set according to the requirements of the exchange rate anchor.

The Mexican *Pacto* and the 1995 ERBS programmes, on the other hand, follow a somewhat different strategy. The *Pacto* had three stages: in the first stage, between February and December 1988, the nominal exchange rate was fixed while nominal wages provided an anchor for inflation. Between January 1989 and November 1991, devaluation was pre-announced and set below the inflation rate under parity. However, the amount by which the currency was led to devalue progressively diminished as the anchor consolidated.

In November 1991, some flexibility was allowed to the exchange rate using a band with a sliding ceiling and flat floor. The band was kept until October 1994 when NAFTA became a considerable issue and pressures from political and other internal developments led to the December 1994 crisis. The crisis required the introduction of a new stabilisation programme in early 1995.

Figure 4.1a: Real exchange rate and inflation gap for Chile

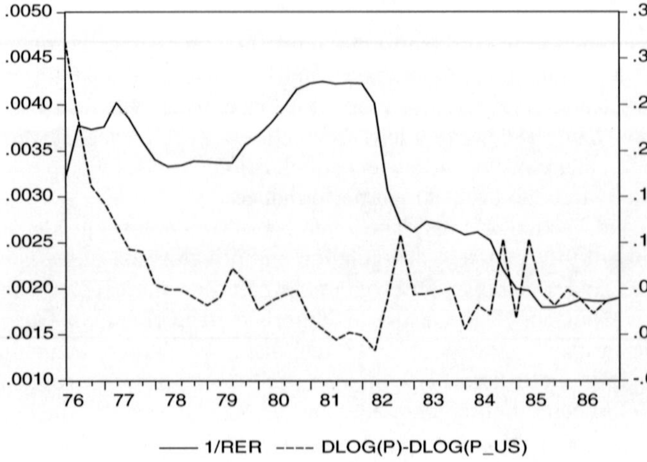

Figure 4.1b: Real exchange rate and inflation gap for Mexico

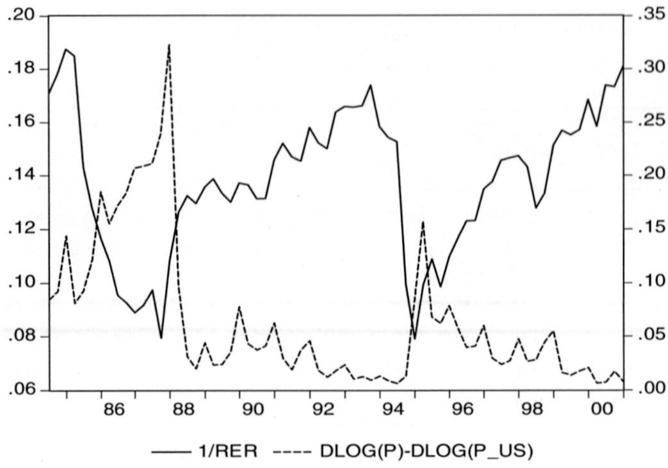

The 1995 programme was an extension of the *Pacto* reinforcing many of the reforms already used in 1977 (see Werner 1994). In particular, 1995 ERBS programme used a nominal exchange rate anchor that was later allowed to grow under parity as the programme consolidated. Contrary to Chile's 1978 programme, both the *Pacto* and the 1995 programmes provided a forward looking mechanism in the formation of wage expectations through the exchange rate target.

As with Chile's backward-looking design, the Mexican forward-looking mechanism did not fully attenuate inertial inflation, causing a significant appreciation of the real exchange rate. Although Chile's real appreciation was substantially higher than Mexico's, it is believed that the reason behind inflation persistence in both countries was the credibility on the nominal anchor (see Figures 4.1a and 4.1b). Edwards (1998) suggests that the Mexican programme was more credible than the Chilean, and as a consequence experienced a relatively less degree of inertia, and a lower real appreciation of the currency. It is not clear, however, whether backward looking wage setting in Chile was directly responsible for the sustained degree of persistence or whether it was the result of credibility in the programme.

Exchange Rate-based Anchors and Inflation Stabilisation

This section develops a model that incorporates the three fundamental hypotheses explaining the appreciation of real exchange rates during the implementation of ERBS programmes. The model accounts for the lack of parameter stability found in the empirical studies on inflation during times of crisis (see Kamin 2001; Fischer 2004).

The analysis shows that these hypotheses are all broadly consistent with a two-good (tradable/non-tradable) rational expectations model with an optimizing social planner that switches preferences in order to achieve stabilisation. In doing so, the model finds that credibility is the central ingredient affecting not only the degree of inertia but also the structural characteristics of the equilibrium real exchange rate.

The model is as follows: this is an open economy that produces tradable and non-tradable goods. Tradable prices are related to international prices under the law of one price such that:

$$\pi_t^T = \delta_t + \pi_t^* \tag{4.1}$$

where π_t^* defines international inflation levels and δ_t is the log change in the nominal exchange rate.[2]

Non-tradable prices are determined by domestic supply and demand. Demand is driven by a measure of non-tradable demand pressures and by a real exchange rate index. Supply is determined by real wages in terms of non-tradable prices. At equilibrium, non-tradable inflation is given by:

$$\pi_t^N = \pi_t^T + \delta_t + \beta_1 w_t + \beta_2 y_t \qquad (4.2)$$

where w_t are nominal wages and y_t is de-trended domestic absorption.[3]

The β's in equation (4.2) are derived from an equilibrium condition in the non-tradable market and are given by $\beta_1 = d_2/(d_1+s_1)$ and $\beta_2 = s_2/(d_1+s_1)$, where $d_1 < 0$ is the price demand elasticity for non-tradable, $d_2 > 0$ is the expenditure elasticity demand for non-tradable, $s_1 < 0$ is the price supply elasticity for non-tradable and $s_2 > 0$ is the real product price supply elasticity for non-tradable.[4]

Agents are forward looking and set wages according to the expected performance of the nominal exchange rate such that:[5]

$$w_t = \varphi E_{t-1}\delta_t \qquad (4.3)$$

where E_t is an expectations operator conditional on the information set and $0 < \varphi \leq 1$.[6]

At the aggregate level, inflation is given by:

---

[2] Henceforward, lowercases denote changes in logarithms.

[3] In Edwards (1992), excess demand pressures are approximated by changes in domestic credit, whereas in Edwards (1998) by de-trended real M2, a measure of excess money demand. In this setup, and following Kamin (2001), excess demand pressures are approximated by de-trended absorption.

[4] The equilibrium condition is defined by $D\left(P^N/P^T \cdot E, Y\right) = S\left(P^T \cdot E/P^N, W\right)$ where the parameters in (4.2) are a combination of supply and demand elasticity after differentiation.

[5] The model is perfectly compatible with backward-looking expectations if wages are set according to past inflation levels. The conclusions of the model are unaffected by this modification.

[6] Equation (4.3) can be rationalize using Dornbusch (1976) such that agents understand the pass through of nominal exchange rates to inflation, working as a forward-looking variable in the formation of expectations.

$$\pi_t = \rho\pi_t^N + (1-\rho)\pi_t^T \tag{4.4}$$

where $0 \le \rho \le 1$ is the relative weight between tradable and non-tradable inflations.

Using equations (4.1) through (4.4), the gap between local and foreign inflation is given by:

$$x_t = E_{t-1}\delta_t + \delta_t + y_{t-1} + \varepsilon_t \tag{4.5}$$

where $x_t = \pi_t - \pi_t^*$.[7]

Regarding exchange rate policy, it is assumed that the central bank follows a real exchange rate target using an index given by:

$$s_t^I = s_{t-1} + \delta_t - x_{t-1} \tag{4.6}$$

where s_t is log of the real exchange rate.[8]

In addition, the model is subject to a game sequence in which the economy is first hit by an external shock, followed by the setting of expectations using all the information available to agents, and finally, a policy response by the central bank.

In an effort to correct inflation and exchange rate misalignments, the central bank adjusts the nominal exchange rate to minimize the following expected objective social loss function:[9]

$$E_{t-1}L_t = E_{t-1}\left[x_t^2 + \lambda\left(s_t^I - s_{t-1}^*\right)^2\right] \tag{4.7}$$

---

[7] Without loss of generality, the coefficients in (4.5) were normalized to unity by setting: $\rho = (1/\varphi) - 1$, $\beta_1 = 1/\rho$ and $\sigma = d_1/d_3$. For simplicity, de-trended domestic absorption is assumed to follows a random walk such that $y_t = y_{t-1} + \varepsilon_t$ where ε_t are *identically and independently distributed* (IID).

[8] The term "real target" is sometimes misleading as it denotes two different types of polices. Some authors refer to it as a *purchasing power parity* (PPP) rule while others define it as a policy aimed at accommodating changes in real exchange rate fundamentals (see Corden 1991). This type of regime has been followed historically by many countries, especially in Latin America (see, for example, Williamson 1981).

[9] The use of a macro welfare function goes back explicitly to Tinbergen (1952). We follow the specification in Barro and Gordon (1983).

where λ measures the relative preferences between inflation and exchange rate targets and s_t^* is the equilibrium real exchange rate which, following Kamin (2001), is a decreasing linear function of *de-trended* domestic absorption:

$$s_t^* = a - by_t \tag{4.8}$$

Following Edwards (1998), a pure ERBS is when the central bank sets $\lambda = 0$. On the other hand, $\lambda > 0$ denotes a *crawling peg* regime. The intensity of the *crawling peg* will increase as $\lambda \to \infty$. For the particular case that $\lambda = 1$, the *crawling peg* is one in which the central bank places equal weights on both inflation and exchange rate misalignments.

In order to understand the effects of regime changes in the form of a stabilisation package and subsequently the role of credibility, the model must be solved under both the *crawling peg* and the ERBS programme. For simplicity, it will be assumed that prior to stabilisation the central bank follows a *crawling peg* with $\lambda = 1$. It is also understood that an ERBS programme implies that $\lambda = 0$. The regime movement from the *crawling peg* to the ERBS will be subject to a probability of success attributed by agents to the stabilisation plan.

Solving Under a Crawling Peg

The problem of the central bank implies minimizing equation (4.7) with respect to δ_t and subject to equations (4.5), (4.6) and (4.8) under the assumption that $\lambda = 1$. The first order condition for the optimization problem is given by:

$$2\delta_t + E_{t-1}\delta_t + s_{t-1} - s_{t-1}^* + y_{t-1} - x_{t-1} + \varepsilon_t = 0 \tag{4.9}$$

From equation (4.9), expectations are given by:

$$E_{t-1}\delta_t = -\frac{1}{3}\left[\left(y_{t-1} - x_{t-1}\right) + \left(s_{t-1} - s_{t-1}^*\right)\right] \tag{4.10}$$

which is decreasing in the gap between lagged inflation and domestic absorption and on the gap between the lagged real exchange rate and its equilibrium level.

From equations (4.9) and (4.10), the nominal exchange rate, which is the policy response of the central bank, becomes:

$$\delta_t = -\frac{1}{3}\left[\left(y_{t-1} - x_{t-1}\right) + \left(s_{t-1} - s^*_{t-1}\right) + \frac{3}{2}\varepsilon_t\right] \tag{4.11}$$

Note that equations (4.10) and (4.11) imply that the model is dynamically consistent. Equation (4.10) indicates that when either output or the real exchange rate exceeds their equilibrium levels, the central bank must correct the exchange rate downwards in order to prevent overheating of the exchange rate.

Substituting (4.10) and (4.11) into (4.5), provides the solution path for inflation under a *crawling peg* regime:

$$x_t^{CP} = \frac{2}{3}x_{t-1} + \frac{2}{3}\left(s_{t-1} - s^*_{t-1}\right) + \frac{1}{3}y_{t-1} + \frac{1}{2}\varepsilon_t \tag{4.12}$$

In order to find the equilibrium/steady state solution for the real exchange rate, equation (4.8) is substituted into (4.12). Setting $x_t^{CP} = 0$, $\varepsilon_t = 0$, and solving for $s_t = s_t^{*CP}\ \forall t$, giving:

$$s_t^{*CP} = a - \frac{1}{2}(2b-1)y_t \tag{4.13}$$

Equation (4.13) is analogous to (4.8) but with the parameter b affecting the slope. In this particular example, the slope will be positive, zero or negative depending on whether b is greater, equal or less than one half $(1/2)$. Equations (4.12) and (4.13) capture the inertial, supply and demand side error corrections forces in explaining the evolution of inflation and the equilibrium real exchange rate.

Solving the Model Under an ERBS Programme

Equations (4.12) and (4.13) say nothing about stabilisation and as a consequence do not provide any useful insights on the effects of these programmes on the evolution of inflation and the real exchange rate. In order to analyse the consequences of stabilisation, the model has to account for the decision of the central bank to engage in a stabilisation programme by evaluating a change of preferences from a *crawling peg* with $\lambda = 1$ to an ERBS with $\lambda = 0$.

Under an ERBS programme, the problem of the central bank implies minimizing equation (4.7) with respect to δ_t and subject to equations (4.5), (4.6) and (4.8), while setting $\lambda = 0$. The first order condition for the optimization problem is given by:

$$E_{t-1}\delta_t + \delta_t + y_{t-1} + \varepsilon_t = 0 \tag{4.14}$$

From equation (4.14), expectations on the policy instrument are given by:

$$E_{t-1}\delta_t = -\frac{1}{2}y_{t-1} \tag{4.15}$$

Equation (4.15) depends on domestic absorption provided that under an ERBS programme the exchange rate is silent or shutdown from the social loss function.

From (4.14) and (4.15), the policy instrument becomes:[10]

$$\delta_t = -\frac{1}{2}\left(y_{t-1} + \varepsilon_t\right) \tag{4.16}$$

The solution path for inflation under ERBS, which results from substituting equations (4.15) and (4.16) into (4.5), is given by:

$$x_t^{ERBS} = 0 \tag{4.17}$$

Equation (4.17) implies that under an ERBS programme, local inflation will immediately converge to international levels. This result is consistent

---

[10] Most variations of these types of models conclude that under an ERBS programme the devaluation rule is to fix the nominal exchange rate if there were no demand-side pressures (see Edwards 1998). For example, if the government uses fiscal stimulus through spending, the optimal reaction of the central bank, according to (4.16), would be to compensate by following a restrictive policy using the exchange rate. If the government is passive by keeping output at its trend, the traditional nominal anchor will be the optimal response. Interestingly, (4.16) provides a rational link between fiscal and monetary policy.

with the fact that the equilibrium real exchange rate will be given by equation (4.8) such that:[11]

$$s_t^{*SP} = a - by_t \tag{4.18}$$

Consequently, the choice of the central bank to engage in a stabilisation programme affects inflation both through inertia as well as through the equilibrium real exchange rate.[12]

Credibility, Inflation and Real Exchange Rates under ERBS

According to the model of sections 4.3.1 and 4.3.2, the transition from a *crawling peg* to an ERBS programme would be instantaneous. However, the stylized facts suggest that inflation usually continues when the nominal exchange rate is used as an anchor, resulting in a real appreciation of the exchange rate (Fischer et al 2002).[13] A way of capturing this inertial effect is by incorporating the concept of credibility.

In doing so, it is assumed that agents placed a probability of $q \in (0,1)$ on the success of the programme. This probability links the pre-stabilisation solution given by equations (4.12) and (4.13), with the post-stabilisation environment given by the equations (4.17) and (4.18). The link provides the dynamics of inflation after the programme is introduced and should behave according to:

$$x_t = (1-q)x_t^{CP} + qx_t^{SP} \tag{4.19}$$

and the equilibrium real exchange rate according to:

---

[11] If there are no demand-side pressures, the equilibrium real exchange rate will be constant and independent from changes in stabilisation preferences and credibility.

[12] This result complies with the literature that emphasizes the role of structural parameter changes in the performance of macroeconomic models (Stock and Watson 1996) and in the design and implementation of macroeconomic policy (Onatski and Williams 2003).

[13] Even if the real exchange rate reaches its equilibrium level relatively fast, it may continue to appreciate if inertial inflation is still high after stabilisation. In this regard, the model will show that a less that fully credible anchor may still cause the real exchange rate to appreciate beyond equilibrium.

$$s_t^* = (1-q)s_t^{*CP} + qs_t^{*SP} \tag{4.20}$$

Substitution of equations (4.12) and (4.17) into (4.19) gives:

$$x_t = \left\{ \frac{2}{3}x_{t-1} + \frac{2}{3}\left(s_{t-1} - s_{t-1}^*\right) + \frac{1}{3}y_{t-1} + \frac{1}{2}\varepsilon_t \right\}(1-q) \tag{4.21}$$

Finally, the equilibrium real exchange rate results from substituting equations (4.13) and (4.18) into (4.20), such that:

$$s_t^* = a - (q + 2b - 1)y_t \tag{4.22}$$

From equations (4.21) and (4.22), inflation and the equilibrium real exchange rate depend on credibility. If agents perceive that the stabilisation programme will not be maintained by attributing a probability $q = 0$, inflation will not be affected by stabilisation. If, however, agents perceived that the programme would succeed by attributing a probability $q = 1$, inflation will instantly converge to international levels.

A more interesting conclusion from the model, however, is that changes in the probability of success will affect the structure of equation (4.22). In this regard, credibility is merging two possible steady states implied by the pre and post stabilisation solutions.

For example, equation (4.22) indicates that for a given level of domestic absorption, the equilibrium real exchange rate will be lower the greater the degree of credibility. Hence, the reduced form relationship between the equilibrium real exchange rate and de-trended domestic absorption will be smaller. This provides a new dimension to the importance of credibility not only as it will affect the degree of inflation, but also by affecting the gap by which the real exchange rate needs to be corrected in order for inflation to stabilize (see the comments in Elliott and Timmermann 2008).

Empirical Evidence

This section tests the implications of the model for Chile and Mexico using recursive regressions. At the empirical level, the central bank would observe and most likely estimate an inflation equation of the form:

$$x_t = \gamma_0 + \gamma_1 x_{t-1} + \gamma_2 s_{t-1} + \gamma_3 y_{t-1} + v_t \tag{4.23}$$

which is an empirical representation of equation (4.21). Using (4.23), the central bank can trace back to find the equilibrium real exchange rate consistent with equation (4.22). In doing so, if the conclusions of the theoretical model are accurate, significant parameter volatility should be expected. Consequently, recursive coefficient techniques should provide information about the evolution of credibility in the stabilisation programme.[14] For example, if q change over time such that $q = q_t$, the estimated coefficients of (4.23) will be recursive and the equilibrium real exchange rate becomes:[15]

$$s_t^* = a - \left(q_t + 2b - 1\right) y_t \tag{4.24}$$

The estimation of equations (4.23) and (4.24) was carried out using quarterly and seasonally adjusted data for real de-trended log industrial production as a proxy of domestic absorption (y);[16] domestic inflation (π), calculated as log changes in the consumer price index (CPI); international inflation, calculated as log changes in the United States (US) CPI (π^*); log changes in the nominal exchange rate (δ) and the log of the real exchange rate (s), calculated as the ratio of the US CPI to local CPI times the nominal 'spot' exchange rate between either Chile or Mexico and the US, such that $P^* E/P$.

For Mexico, the data ranges from the first quarter of 1981 up to first quarter of 2001, which includes the *Pacto* stabilisation programme implemented in January of 1988 and the 1994 *Tequila* crisis. For Chile, the data ranges from the first quarter of 1971 up to the first quarter of 1988, including the 1978 ERBS programme and the 1983 currency crisis.

Table 4.1 tests the integration consistency of the series using the ADF test for stationarity (Dickey and Fuller 1979). The results show that in both countries the inflation gap and de-trended industrial production follow I(0) process. However, the real exchange rate follows a first order-integrated process providing additional evidence of the integration consistency of the model.

---

[14] The analysis also looks at the evolution of inflation inertia and its relationship to credibility. This has been well documented for Chile and Mexico in Edwards (1996) and Edwards (1998).

[15] In a more general setting, credibility should be endogenous reflecting reputation levels, electoral cycles, and policy performance (see Prazmowski 2002).

[16] Absorption de-trending was carried out using the Hodrick and Prescott (1997) filter.

Table 4.1: ADF test

Variable	Chile[a]	Mexico[b]
x	-4.38**	-2.9*
s	-0.83	-1.94
Δs	-3.87*	-6.96**
y	-4.05**	-3.43*

Note: * and ** denote significance at the 1% and 5% level under MacKinnon (1991) critical surface. The data is available by request to the authors.
(a) Estimation sample is 1981.1-2000.1
(b) Estimation sample is 1981.1-2001.1

Figures 4.2a and 4.2b compares the real exchange rate and *de-trended* industrial production for Chile and Mexico. The graphs illustrate that the reciprocal of the real exchange rate and de-trended industrial production are highly correlated providing support for cointegration as implied by equation (4.24). The result indicates that reductions in output tend to appreciate the currency while causing inflation.

Table 4.2, on the other hand, shows the estimation of equation (4.23) for Chile and Mexico.[17] For this exercise, Mexico appears to have substantially higher inflation inertia than Chile (0.79 vs. 0.62), although unit root tests reject a random walk in both cases, providing evidence of average mean reversion. Alternatively, Figures 4.3a and 4.3b show the recursive *time-varying coefficients* (TVC) for lagged inflation.[18]

[17] The fact that there are no contemporaneous endogenous variables in equation (4.23) rules out any simultaneity bias in the estimation by using *Ordinary Least Square* (OLS) (see Hamilton 1994).

[18] In the TVC solution or recursive least squares, a time series of coefficient estimates is obtained using an updating algorithm in which the equation is estimated using the first k observations, in which k is the number of parameters to be estimated, and new observations are added until the full sample is used, obtaining T-k+1 coefficient estimates.

Figure 4.2a: 1/RER and de-trended industrial production (Chile)

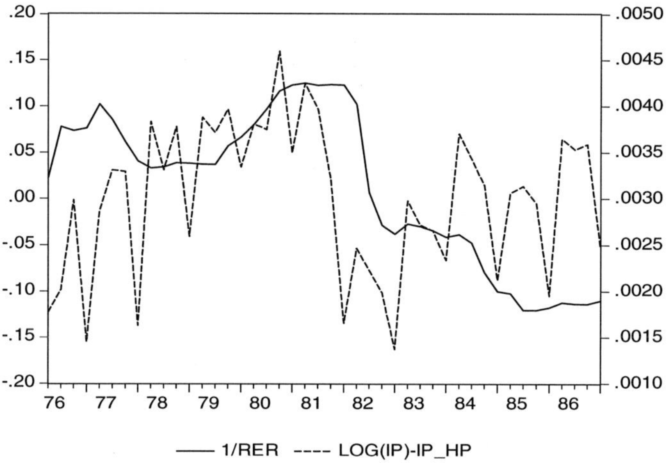

Figure 4.2b: 1/RER and de-trended industrial production (Mexico)

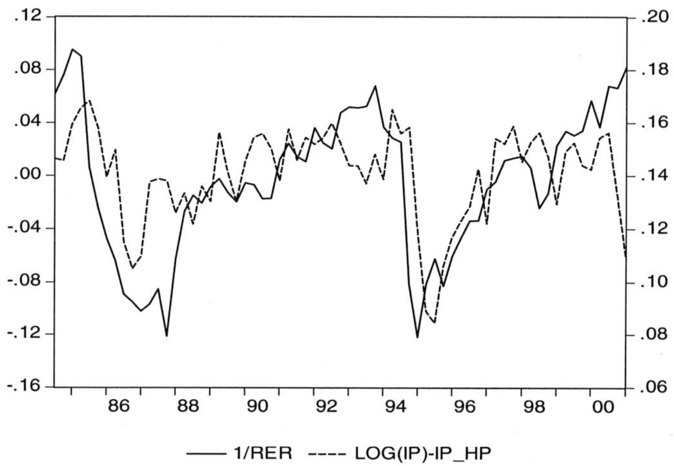

Table 4.2: Regression results for the inflation gap

Variable	Coefficient	Chile[b]	Mexico[b]
Constant	ζ_0	0.72*	-0.14*
		(0.17)	(0.05)
x_{t-1}	ζ_1	0.62*	0.79*
		(0.08)	(0.16)
s_{t-1}	ζ_2	-0.12*	0.08*
		(0.03)	(0.03)
y_{t-1}	ζ_3	-0.27**	0.41*
		(0.11)	(0.14)
R2 (adjusted)		0.75	0.72
N (adjusted)		61	79
σ2 (ρεγρεσσιον)		0.08	0.04
DW-h		2.03	1.77
ADF		-2.72*	-7.75*

Note: * and ** denote significance at the 1% and 5% level respectively.
(a) Estimation sample is 1971.1-1988.1
(b) Estimation sample is 1981.1-2001.1
Estimation using White's (1980) Heteroskedasticity-consistent cavariance.

Table 4.3: Johansen test for RER and de-trended IP

Country	Chile[b]		Mexico[a]	
Eigenvalue	0.20*	0.06	0.47*	0.13
Null hypothesis	r = 0 r = 1	r = 1 r = 2	r = 0 r = 1	r = 1 r = 2
φ_{trace}	21.42	4.80	41.18	7.40
φ_{trace} 95% critical value	19.96	9.24	19.96	9.24
φ_{trace} 99% critical value	24.60	12.97	24.60	12.97
Null hypothesis	r = 0 r > 1	r ≤ 1 r > 1	r = 0 r > 1	r ≤ 1 r > 1
φ_{max}	16.62	4.80	33.78	7.40
φ_{max} 95% critical value	15.67	9.24	15.67	9.24
φ_{max} 99% critical value	20.20	12.97	20.20	12.97

Note: * and ** denote rejection of the hypothesis at the 1% and 5% level under Osterwald-Lenum (1992) critical surface. The statistics φ_{trace} and φ_{max} are the trace and maximal eigenvalues under Johansen (1991) cointegration test.
(a) Vector autoregression includes constant term. Estimation sample is 1988.1-2000.1
(b) Vector autoregression includes constant term. Estimation sample is 1981.1-2001.1

Figure 4.3a: Inflation inertia in Chile

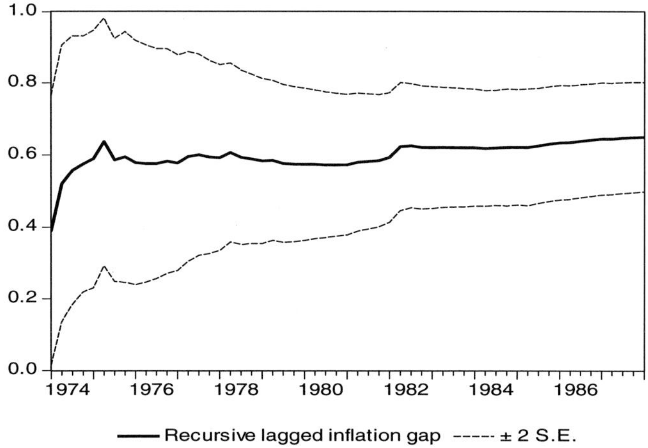

Figure 4.3b: Inflation inertia in Mexico

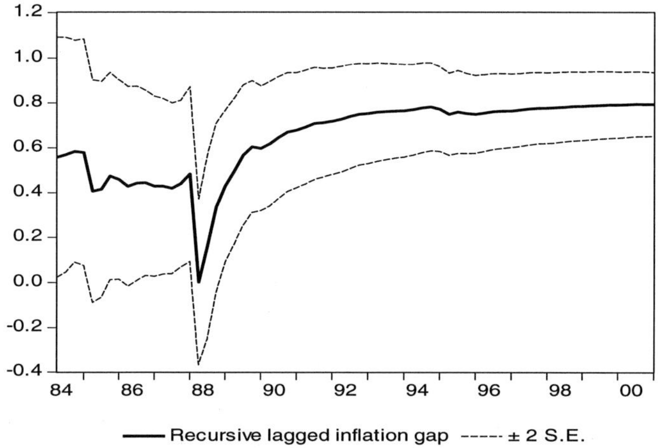

For Chile, there was no significant reduction in inertia after the introduction of the stabilisation programme neither in February 1978 nor during its modification in June 1979. In fact, inertia gradually continued during the implementation and consolidation of the programme. On the contrary, México shows a clear drop in inertia at the time the exchange rate anchor was adopted in 1988. The drop in inertia was sustained until January 1989, when it reverted to pre-stabilisation levels.

It is not entirely clear from the theoretical analysis, however, that movements in inertia are entirely due to credibility. The reason is that there were different wage indexation schemes that may have affected the inertia profile in both countries. Chile had a formal backward-looking indexation while in Mexico, the exchange rate anchor provided a forward-looking mechanism in the formation of wage expectations. It is plausible that the backward looking mechanism in Chile could have fuelled inflation inertia even under a credible anchor (see Edwards 1998). In Mexico, which had a forward-looking expectations mechanism, the observed drop in inertia could be attributed to a credibility effect.[19] According to the model, this question can be answered by looking at the parameters changes in the equilibrium real exchange rate.

Table 4.2 can be used to trace back and obtain the empirical representation of equilibrium real exchange rate (equation 4.23). This requires, however, that the real exchange rate and domestic de-trended absorption be co-integrated. In doing so, an ADF tests on the residuals for both countries indicate that they are stationary at the 1 per cent level which according to the Engle and Granger (1987) is a necessary condition for co-integration. The Johansen (1991) test in Table 4.3 also confirms the existence of at least one co-integrated relationship in both cases. For Mexico, the normalized equilibrium real exchange rate is given by:[20]

$$s_t^* = \underset{(0.34)}{1.79} - \underset{(2.74)}{5.10}\, y_t \qquad (4.25)$$

and for Chile is given by:

$$s_t^* = \underset{(2.57)}{6.05} - \underset{(0.81)}{2.26}\, y_t \qquad (4.26)$$

[19] The TVC analysis of the equilibrium exchange rate obtained from the estimation of equation (4.23) confirms that the exchange rate anchor in Chile lacks credibility while the one in Mexico had a clear credibility effect.

[20] Equations (4.25) and (4.26), and any equilibrium real exchange rate thereof, can be calculated by equating local inflation to world inflation, setting the growth rate of the nominal exchange rate to zero and then isolating the real exchange rate in the results of Table 4.2 for each country. The standard error (in parenthesis) is calculated using
$\mathrm{var}(\hat{\varphi}_j/\hat{\varphi}_1) \cong (1/\hat{\varphi})^2\, \mathrm{var}(\hat{\varphi}_j) + (\hat{\varphi}_j/\hat{\varphi}_1)^2\, \mathrm{var}(\hat{\varphi}_1) + 2(1/-\hat{\varphi})(\hat{\varphi}_j/\hat{\varphi}_1)\,\mathrm{cov}(\hat{\varphi}_1, \hat{\varphi}_j)$,
for $j = 1, 3$. See Bårdsen (1989) for details.

Equations (4.25) and (4.26) are the empirical representation of equation (4.22) in Section 4.2. Note that in Mexico, the intercept is higher than in Chile and the slope is smaller. Using the theoretical model, this can be interpreted as follows:

Firstly, a was higher in Chile implying that in the absence of demand-side pressures, the equilibrium real exchange rate consistent with inflation stability is on average higher. Secondly, the slope coefficient is smaller in Mexico perhaps because the parameter b is smaller or because average credibility (q) was higher.

According to equation (4.22), changes in this coefficient are entirely due to credibility. As a consequence, the TVC of the slope of the equilibrium real exchange rate can provide a less contaminated estimate of the evolution of credibility than the TVC on inertial inflation. Figures 4.4a and 4.4b show the TVC of the slope of equations (4.25) and (4.26). An increase in absolute value indicates a drop in credibility and a fall in absolute value indicate an improvement in credibility.

After February 1978, when Chile announced its stabilisation programme with the formal backward-looking wage setting scheme and the nominal anchor was left to devalue under parity, the slope coefficient started to increase in absolute value indicating that the programme lost credibility.

Figure 4.4a: TVC slope of normalized ECM for Chile

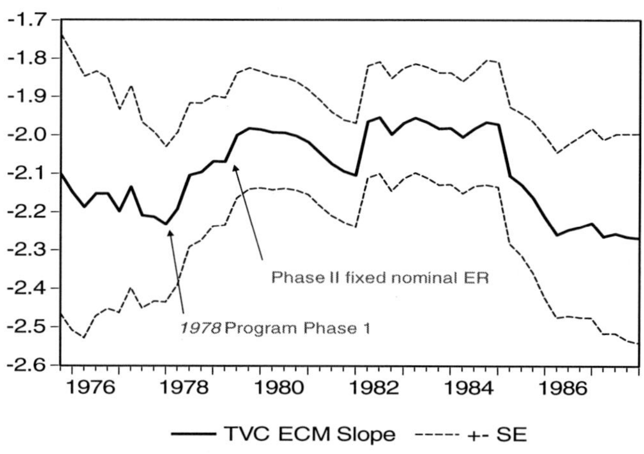

Interestingly, the loss of credibility continued until June 1979 when the second phase of the programme was implemented with a fixed nominal exchange rate at 39 pesos per dollar. The graph shows that after the second quarter of 1979, some credibility was regained until 1982 when the nominal anchor was lost and the currency collapsed.

For Mexico, the story is somewhat different. After the introduction of the *Pacto* programme in February 1988, with a fixed nominal exchange rate that lasted until December of that same year, the slope coefficient dropped significantly, showing a considerable credibility effect.

Starting in January of 1989, when the central bank pre-announced and allowed the exchange rate to devalue under parity, the slope coefficient started to increase, indicating a gradual loss of credibility. The drop in credibility continued past December 1994 when NAFTA and other local developments caused a collapse of the anchor and a devaluation of the currency.

The introduction of the 1995 ERBS programme was much more successful, as indicated by the significant drop in the TVC, showing evidence of a strong credibility effect. It is important to recall that the main feature of the 1995 programme was a fixing of the nominal exchange rate similar to the initial phase of 1988 programme and perhaps contributing to this credibility.

Figure 4.4b: TVC slope of normalized ECM for Mexico

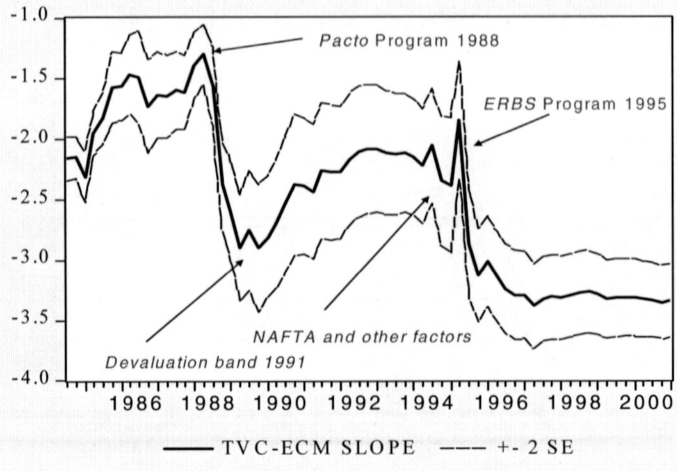

Figure 4.5a: Observed vs. equilibrium RER (constant and TVC for Chile)

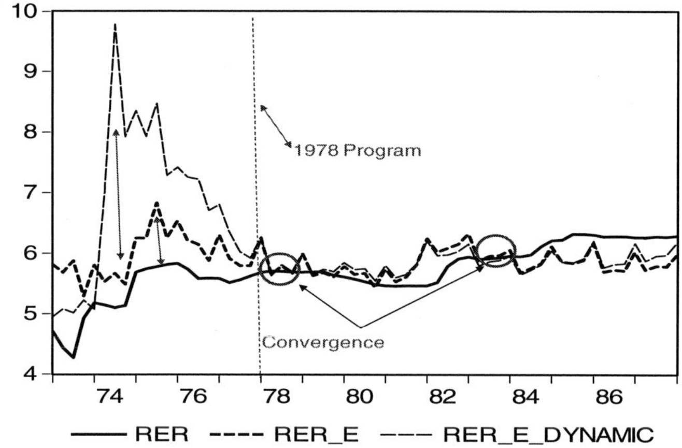

Figure 4.5b: Observed vs. equilibrium RER (constant and TVC for Mexico)

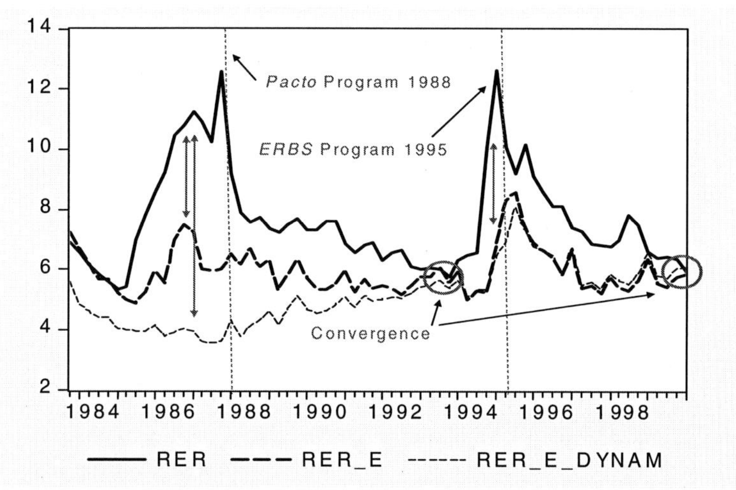

A central conclusion from these results is that credibility about the stabilisation programme is closely related to the way in which the central bank sets the nominal anchor. It appears that fixing the currency under an ERBS programme provides more credibility than a soft band such as Chile's 1978 programme or Mexico's first phase of 1988. This can be rationalized, perhaps because a soft band may signal less commitment on the central bank with respect to the stabilisation programme.

Policy Implications

If the central bank uses the equilibrium real exchange rate to implement inflation and exchange rate stabilisation polices, and in doing so ignores the structural changes implied by the model, the conclusions can be dramatically misleading as the equilibrium gap consistent with inflation stability can be substantially different.

To understand this argument, the real exchange rate calculated using TVC is compared with the end of sample constant coefficient case (CCC). Figures 4.5a and 4.5b contrast the actual real exchange rate with the TVC and the CCC estimate for Chile and Mexico. The figures illustrate that the equilibrium using TVC is substantially different from the CCC. This difference is more relevant during times of crisis.

In particular, after taking into consideration the TVC, the real exchange rate appears to be more depreciated than the CCC equilibrium suggested at the time the stabilisation programme was introduced. As a consequence, in order to achieve inflation stabilisation, all else equal, the real exchange rate needed to appreciate more than the CCC would have suggested. For both Chile and Mexico, the TVC and CCC differ substantially. These findings imply a serious bias in the calculation of the equilibrium real exchange rate when the TVC is ignored.

For Mexico, equilibrium was partially achieved in the first quarter of 1991, lost again during the 1994 Tequila crisis and regained after the second quarter of 1995. For Chile, equilibrium was partially achieved when the stand-by agreement was announced in October 1990, and fully reached when the programme was formally introduced in the third quarter of 1991. Equilibrium was lost between 1993 and 1995, which according to the TVC method, was partially restored afterwards. Although both equilibrium estimates move in a similar fashion, the equilibrium gap varies substantially depending to the methodology used. In general, structural dynamics matter in the evolution of equilibrium especially during times of substantial volatility.

Conclusion

This chapter proposes a framework that allows understanding the implications of regime changes and credibility in the evolution of inflation and the equilibrium real exchange rate during stabilisation. The analysis show that changes in credibility, in the form of a programme's success probabilities, affects inertial inflation and will influence the parameters of the equilibrium real exchange rate. Consequently, understanding credibility is crucial to evaluating the performance of the stabilisation plan. The hypothesis is empirically tested for Chile and Mexico stabilisation episodes using a recursive TVC technique.

The results suggest that Chile's 1978 stabilisation effort lacked credibility in its first phase mainly because the central bank introduced a programme that had a flexible exchange rate anchor. The programme gained credibility in a second phase, however, because it reverted to a fixed nominal anchor. On the contrary, the 1988 *Pacto* programme in Mexico had a significant credibility effect in its first phase mainly because the central bank introduced a fixed nominal anchor, although, the programme lost credibility when the monetary authorities allowed the exchange rate anchor to slide under parity. The 1995 programme in Mexico was perhaps the most successful because it maintained a fixed nominal target.

The results suggest that the way in which the central bank manages the nominal anchor under an ERBS programme will substantially affect credibility on the stabilisation attempt and hence the dynamics of inflation and the real exchange rate. Structural changes can provide important information about the performance of the stabilisation programme and, if ignored, could deceive the authorities in the implementation of successful inflation and exchange rate policies.

References

Bårdsen, G., 1989, The Estimation of Long-Run Coefficients from Error Correction Models, *Oxford Bulletin of Economics and Statistics*, 54, 345-50.

Barro, R. J., and D. B. Gordon, 1983, A Positive Theory of Monetary Policy in a Natural-Rate Model, *Journal of Political Economy*, 91 (August), 589-610.

Calvo, G., and C. A. Végh, 1993, Exchange Rate Based Stabilization under Imperfect Credibility, in H. Frisch and A. Worgotter (eds.) *Open Economy Macroeconomics*, MacMillan, 3-28.

—. 1999, Inflation Stabilization and BOP Crises in Developing Countries, in Taylor, J.B. and M. Woodford, (eds.), *Handbook of Macroeconomics*, 1, 1531–1614.

Corden, W.M., 1991, Macroeconomic Policy and Growth: Some Lessons of Experience, in Proceedings of the World Bank Annual Conference on Development Economics, *The Economic Journal*, 1, 1531–1614.

Dickey, D. A., and W. A. Fuller, 1979, Distribution of the Estimators for Autoregressive Time Series with a Unit Root, *Journal of the American Statistical Association*, 74, 427-431.

Dornbusch, R., 1976, Expectations and Exchange Rate Dynamics, *Journal of Political Economy*, 84 (December), 1161-1176.

Dornbusch, R., and A. Werner, 1994, Mexico: Stabilization, Reform and No Growth, *Brookings Papers on Economic Activity*, 1, 253-315.

Edwards, S., 1992, Exchange Rates as Nominal Anchors, *NBER* 4246.

—. 1996, Exchange Rate Anchors, Credibility and Inertia: A Tale of Two Crises: Chile and Mexico, *American Economic Review*, 86 (2), 176-180.

—. 1998, Two Crises: Inflationary Inertia and Credibility, *The Economic Journal*, 108, 665-80.

Elliott, G. and A. Timmermann, 2008, Economic Forecasting, *Journal of Economic Literature*, 46, 3-56.

Engle, R. F., and C. W. J. Granger, 1987, Co-integration and Error Correction: Representation, Estimation, and Testing, *Econometrica*, 55, 251-276.

Erceg, C.J., and A.T. Levin, 1996, Structures Investment and the Dynamic Behaviour of the Real Exchange Rate, *Board of Governors of the Federal Reserve System*, Washington, DC.

Fischer, S., 2004, *IMF Essays from a Time of Crisis*, MIT Press.

Fischer, S., R. Sahay, and C. A. Végh, 2002, Modern Hyper and High Inflations, *Journal of Economic Literature*, 40, 837-880.

Gil-Diaz, F., and A. Carstens, 1996, One Year of Solitude: Some Pilgrim Tales about Mexico's 1994-1995 Crisis, *American Economic Review*, 82 (2), 164-169.

Hamilton, J. D., 1994, *Time Series Analysis*, Princeton University Press.

Hodrick, R. J., and E. C., Prescott, 1997, Post-war U.S. Business Cycles: An Empirical Investigation, *Journal of Money, Credit, and Banking*, 29, 1-16.

Onatski, A. and N. Williams, 2003, Modeling Model Uncertainty, *Journal of the European Economic Association*, 1, 1087-1022.

Johansen, S., 1991, Estimation and Hypothesis Testing of Co-integration Vectors in Gaussian Vector Autoregressive Models, *Econometrica*, 59, 1551-1580.

Kamin, S. B., 2001, Real Exchange Rates and Inflation in Exchange-Rate-Based Stabilizations: An Empirical Examination, *Journal of Development Economics*, 64, 237-253.

Lucas, R., 1976, Econometric Policy Evaluation: A Critique, *Carnegie-Rochester Conference Series on Public Policy*, 1, 19-46.

MacKinnon, J., 1991, Critical Values for Cointegration Tests, Chapter 13 in R. F., Engle and C. W., Granger (eds.), *Long-Run Economic Relationships*, Oxford University Press.

Meese, R. A. and K. Rogo, 1983b, The Out-of-Sample Failure of Empirical Exchange Rate Models: Sampling Error or Misspecification? in J. Frenkel (eds.), *Exchange Rates and International Macroeconomics*, University of Chicago Press, 67-105,.

Osterwald-Lenum, M., 1992, A Note with Quintiles of the Asymptotic Distribution of the Maximum Likelihood Cointegration Rank Test Statistics, *Oxford Bulletin of Economics and Statistics*, 54, 461-472.

Prazmowski, P. A., 2002, Endogenous Credibility and Stabilization Programs: Evidence from the Dominican Republic, *Applied Economics Letters*, 9, 933-937.

Rebelo, S., and C. A., Végh, 1994, Real Effects of Exchange Rate Based Stabilization: An Analysis of Competing Theories, *NBER Macroeconomics Annual*, 125-74.

Rodríguez, C. A., 1982, The Argentine Stabilization Plan of December 20th, *World Development*, 10, 801-11.

Stock, James, H. and M. W. Watson, 1996, Evidence on Structural Instability in Macroeconomic Time Series Relations, *Journal of Business and Economic Statistics* 14, 11-30.

Tinbergen, J., 1952, *On the Theory of Economic Policy*, North-Holland.

Werner, A., 1994, Mexico: Stabilization, Reform and No Growth, *Brooking Papers in Economic Activity*, l, 253-315.

Williamson, J., 1981, *Exchange Rate Rules: The Theory, Performance and Prospects of the Crawling Peg*., St. Martin's Press.

White, H., 1980, A Heteroskedasticity-Consistent Covariance Matrix and a Direct Test for Heteroskedasticity, *Econometrica*, 48, 817-838.

CHAPTER FIVE

MEASURING THE TIMING OF STABILISATION

Introduction

The timing of stabilisation plans is of relevance as it may have significant welfare implications. The literature dealing with this subject uses the concept of duration to measure both the reaction of the authorities when implementing a stabilisation programme as well as the effectiveness of the programmes in controlling inflation.

There are two types of duration: The first, known as delays in stabilisation, calculates the difference between the date in which the economy reaches some threshold definition of high inflation and the actual date in which the central bank formally implements a stabilisation programme. The second, known as a stabilisation episode, is the difference between the date on which the central bank implements the programme and when the economy reaches some definition of inflation stability.[1] Consequently, the delays in stabilisation measure the agility of the central bank when engaging in stabilisation attempts while a stabilisation episode measures the success of the programme.

Some authors, such as Ball (1994), propose rules for measuring duration based on inflation multiples. For example, Easterly (1996) defines an inflation crisis as a period of at least two consecutive years with inflation above 40 per cent, and a non-crisis state as a period of at least two consecutive years with inflation below 40 per cent. Duration is the difference between the actual date of stabilisation and these threshold definitions of high and low inflation. The problem, however, is that these threshold definitions have been highly criticized as mechanical and

---

[1] It is often argued that welfare improving stabilisation policies in countries suffering from chronic inflation are delayed or not fully implemented because of coordination problems that arise from bargaining games between agents and governments (see, for example, Alesina 1994; Drazen 1996; Rodrick 1993; Rodrick 1996). It is also argued that political opportunism affects the timing of stabilisation (see Alesina and Tabellini 1990; Persson and Svensson 1989).

arbitrary (see Hamann 2001). This chapter proposes a model to account for the implications of regime changes in shaping stabilisation programmes, aiming at deriving a welfare-improving stabilisation rule that could replace these traditional threshold definitions of high and low inflation. The rule uses a conditional variance or volatility condition that overshoots at or near the dates in which the economy enters a crisis state and that returns to negligible levels when stability is regained. Duration for the delays in implementing stabilisation and dose for achieving a stabilisation episode is calculated using an *Autoregressive Conditional Heteroskedasticity* (ARCH) model that follows Engle (1982) conditional variance specification.

The results reveal that, in the context of the open economy, the decision to introduce a stabilisation plan will depend on the variance of inflation. In particular, the analysis shows that if the variance of inflation is significantly large, a central bank could benefit from adopting a nominal anchor in the context of a formal stabilisation programme. Contrary to other frameworks, this approach is based on a rational, forward-looking central bank that maximizes social welfare by looking the variance of inflation in an effort to determine the optimal time to engage in a stabilisation programme

The analysis is novel and provides an alternative and arguably more rigorous approach for calculating duration in stabilisation. Secondly, the conclusions derived from the model alongside the historical accounts of countries engaging in stabilisation programmes reveal the existence of *heteroskedasticity*, providing a reasonable argument for using conditional variance or ARCH models in the analysis of inflation, specially in countries that have a history of stabilisation attempts. In these cases analysis can also be used to determine the degree of externalities, in the form of coordination failure and political opportunism, which could be creating delays in stabilization. Finally, the analysis could assist central bankers in the decision to engage in stabilisation and for evaluating the effectiveness of the programmes in controlling inflation.

The rest of the chapter is as follows: Section 5.2 develops the analytical model and advances a set of formal hypotheses. Section 5.3 carries out an empirical exercise on a sample of developing countries that have adopted *International Monetary Fund* (IMF) *exchange rate-based stabilisation* (ERBS) programmes and tests the model alongside the proposed hypothesis. Section 5.4 uses the models in calculating duration for delays and stabilisation episodes. Section 5.5 concludes.

A Model of Welfare Driven Stabilisation

This section extends Edwards (1998) by developing a model to evaluate the conditions under which ERBS programmes are welfare-improving. The welfare-improving condition is derived from a central bank that minimizes a quadratic loss function in an environment subject to forward looking wage indexation. Within this framework, the adoption of a stabilisation plan is interpreted as a change in the authorities' preferences moving from a *crawling peg* regime to a fully fledged nominal exchange rate anchor in the form of a stabilisation programme.[2]

Formally, it is assumed that the central bank dislikes both inflation and real exchange rate misalignments as represented by the following social loss function:

$$L_t = \left(x_t - x_t^*\right)^2 + \lambda\left(s_t - s_t^*\right)^2 \tag{5.1}$$

where, $x_t = \pi_t - \pi_t^*$ is the gap between local and international inflation levels, s_t is the log change in the real exchange rate, $s_t^* = \varepsilon_t$ measures the changes in the target or equilibrium real exchange rate, assumed to be affected in every period by an *independent and identically distributed* (IID term-of-trade) shock, and λ measures the relative preferences between inflation and real exchange rate targets.[3]

In this framework, a *crawling peg* regime is a situation in which the central bank puts more weight on real exchange rate misalignments by setting $\lambda > 0$. Conversely, an ERBS programme is a situation in which the central bank is entirely concerned in avoiding inflation differentials and sets $\lambda = 0$.

Prior to stabilisation, the central bank is assumed to follow a *crawling peg* regime using a real exchange rate index defined by:

$$s_t = \delta_t - \theta x_{t-j} \tag{5.2}$$

[2] The success of the programme will depend on the extent by which a change in preferences is credible. However, in the context on this model, it will be assumed that the central bank enjoys full credibility in the conduct of macroeconomic policy.

[3] Other sensible assumptions can be made regarding the behaviour of the equilibrium real exchange rate. For example, in Kamin (2001) the equilibrium real exchange rate is as a decreasing function in de-trended domestic absorption whereas in Edwards (1998) the equilibrium real exchange rate is constant.

where $\theta \leq 1$ measures the relative importance that the central bank places on inflation differentials when evaluating exchange rate policy. This type of real exchange rate rule, in which central banks look at lagged inflation to adjust their nominal exchange rate, has been followed in many developing countries. If $\theta < 1$, the nominal exchange rate is adjusted by less than inflation differentials. When $\theta = 1$ and $j = 0$ equation (5.2) becomes the traditional real exchange rate index. In this model, I follow Williamson (1981) by setting $\theta = 1$ and Edwards (1996) by setting $j = 1$. The central bank is assumed to control δ_t, which measures the changes in the nominal exchange rate.

Finally, this is an open economy that produces tradable and non-tradable goods. Tradable prices are related to international prices via the law of one price and non-tradable prices are determined by domestic supply and demand. Wages are based on expected inflation. Aggregate inflation is thus defined as a weighted average of tradable and non-tradable prices.

Under rational expectations, the resulting resource balance for this economy is given by:[4]

$$x_t = \delta_t \tag{5.3}$$

The solution of the model is carried out by minimizing equation (5.1) with respect to δ_t and subject to equations (5.2) and (5.3). The optimal devaluation rule resulting from the central bank's optimization problem is given by:

---

[4] Specifically, non-tradable inflation, which is derived from an equilibrium condition in the non-tradable goods market, is given by: $\pi_t^N = \beta_1 \pi_t^* + \beta_2 w_t + \beta_3 z_t$, where π_t^N is non-tradable inflation, π_t^* is foreign inflation, w_t is the change in the log of nominal wages, and z_t is a measure of excess demand pressures. The coefficients in the non-tradable inflation equation depend on the underlying elasticity of supply and demand, which under reasonable assumptions should be positive. For convenience, and without loss of generality, these coefficients have been normalized to unity. The central bank is also assumed to correct any excess demand pressures from the system. Inflation of tradable prices is given by: $\pi_t^T = \delta_t + \pi_t^*$, and wage inflation by: $w_t = E(\pi_t)$, where E is an expectations operator conditional on all past available information (see Edwards 1998 for a derivation of a similar model).

$$\delta_t = \frac{\lambda}{1+\lambda}\left(x_t + \varepsilon_t\right) \tag{5.4}$$

Equation (5.4) depends on the type of regime chosen. If $\lambda = 0$ the nominal exchange rate will be anchored and set to zero. If $\lambda > 0$ and a *crawling peg* is followed, the nominal exchange rate will be adjusted according to exogenous shocks and past inflation differentials.

After substituting equation (5.4) back into (5.1) and (5.2), it follows that the paths of inflation and the real exchange rate are given by:

$$x_t = \frac{\lambda}{1+\lambda} x_{t-1} + \frac{\lambda}{1+\lambda} \varepsilon_t \tag{5.5}$$

$$s_t = -\frac{1}{1+\lambda} x_{t-1} + \frac{\lambda}{1+\lambda} \varepsilon_t \tag{5.6}$$

Under an ERBS programme with $\lambda = 0$, the central bank will control inflation such that $x_t = 0$ and the real exchange rate will converge to parity as $s_t = -x_t$. In both equations, the stabilisation programme eliminates the volatility coming from term-of-trade shocks. However, how much volatility is fed back into the model depends on the chosen value of λ. The greater the level of λ the larger will be the effects of trade shocks on inflation and the stronger the persistence of inflation on a real appreciation of the currency. Intuitively, a rational choice of the central bank when volatility shocks are large is to engage in a stabilisation programme by setting $\lambda = 0$.

This can be formally demonstrated by evaluating the welfare implications of changes in stabilisation preferences. Substitution of equations (5.5) and (5.6) into (5.1) and taking expectations gives:

$$E\left(L_t\right) = \varphi + \frac{\lambda}{1+\lambda} Var\left(\varepsilon_t\right) \tag{5.7}$$

where, $\varphi = \left(\lambda/1+\lambda\right) x_{t-1}^2$ is a *non-diversifiable* social loss level resulting from previous inflation differentials. Equation (5.7) is based on the assumption that $\varepsilon_t \sim N\left[0, Var\left(\varepsilon_t\right)\right]$ where $Var\left(\varepsilon_t\right) \geq 0$. Consequently, a regime change will be welfare improving if and only if:

$$\frac{\partial E(L_t)}{\partial \lambda} \equiv \frac{Var(\varepsilon_t)}{(1+\lambda)^2} < 0 \tag{5.8}$$

Given that $Var(\varepsilon_t) \geq 0$, condition (5.8) states that movements towards a nominal exchange rate anchor under an ERBS programme (i.e. $\partial\lambda < 0$) will improve social welfare if and only if the variance of inflation is positive.[5] A positive variance is the result of persistent shocks to the economy. As a consequence, when prices are subject to volatility, it is in society's best interests that the central bank moves toward a nominal anchor around a formal stabilisation programme for controlling inflation.[6]

Nonetheless, and following Levy-Yeyati and Sturzenegger's (2001) *fear of pegging*, it is unlikely that the authorities will move to a strict ERBS when condition (5.8) bites. As a consequence, it is plausible that once inflation stabilizes, the authorities will revert their preferences towards a *crawling peg* scenario with higher values of λ. This situation will reintroduce volatility into the system, thus requiring a new stabilisation attempt. Incidentally, the story does comply with the history of repeated stabilisation episodes that have characterized many developing countries (see Edwards 1996).[7]

Another important aspect of the model is that the concavity of the loss function implies that the further back that the central bank stands at the time when condition (5.8) suggests a stabilisation programme, the greater will be the welfare gains associated with a change of preferences towards

---

[5] Condition (5.8) assumes that the central bank only cares about the expected shocks when evaluating changes in stabilisation preferences. In this regard, past inflation differentials, when positive, are regarded as non-diversifiable and related to already realized preference levels as represented by φ. Changes in preferences will only be subject to what the central bank can achieve in the future as new preferences could be adjusted to minimize social loss while taking past inflation differentials as given.

[6] There are numerous extensions to the model that can introduce a covariance term in equations (5.7) such that condition (5.8) can become negative if the covariance is negative and large. This will allow situations in which the model suggests reverting back to a *crawling peg* regime.

[7] A similar story can be told when the stabilisation programme loses credibility such as in Sargent (1982). In this case, the value of λ is subject to a probability of success attributed by agents. If the public perceives that the central bank will be unable to manage the programme, the probability of success falls and λ reverts back to pre-stabilisation levels, allowing shocks back in the systems, creating volatility and thus requiring a new stabilisation programme.

stabilisation policies. In addition, the larger the $Var(\varepsilon_t)$ the greater will be the social loss associated with delaying the stabilisation plan. The value of $Var(\varepsilon_t)$ thus defines the direction and timing for a regime change towards a stabilisation programme in general and ERBS in particular.

Figure 5.1 provides a graphical description of the regime-shifting condition. The graphs displays the expected social loss and its derivative, equations (5.7) and (5.8), alongside the optimal movement towards stabilisation. It shows that when $Var(\varepsilon_t) > 0$, the derivative of the loss function with respect to regime preferences is always positive and preferences should move towards lower values of λ in order to reduce social losses. At $\lambda = 0$ welfare losses are minimized.

Figure 5.1: Expected social loss and regime changes

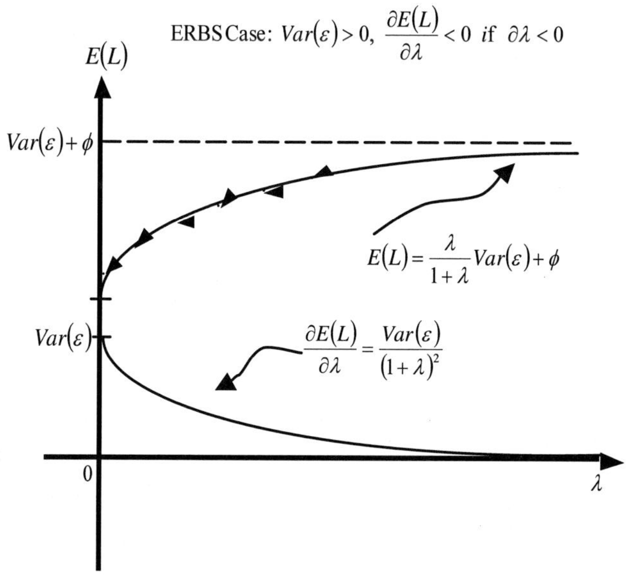

Heteroskedasticity and Stabilisation

This section puts forward a hypothesis stating that inflation in countries that have a history of stabilisation attempts should be *heteroskedastic*. It also establishes that a conditional variance or volatility model can be used to determine the optimal timing of stabilisation plans.

In particular, history suggests that countries go in and out of stabilisation. For example, Table 5.1 shows a sample of 6 Latin American countries, namely Argentina, Brazil, Chile, Mexico, Peru and Uruguay that between 1970 and 2004 have engaged in more than 17 ERBS programmes altogether.[8]

If the model in section 5.3 captures the response of the central bank adopting stabilisation plans, and this decision is based on the variance of inflation, the model in this chapter suggests that this variance changes over time, implying *heteroskedasticity*. Given that *heteroskedasticity* is formally studied using conditional variance or volatility models, the following proposition should hold: Inflation processes, in countries with a history of stabilisation attempts, must be *heteroskedastic* and can be approximated by a conditional variance ARCH model (Engle, 1982).

In addition, it can be expected that the ARCH of the inflation process must coincide with stabilisation attempts, overshooting at or near the days a central bank implements the stabilisation programme. Specifically, the hypothesis states that inflation processes in countries that have a history of stabilisation attempts should have a significantly positive conditional volatility component that matches up with the dates in which these countries have engaged in ERBS programmes. This result is due to the fact that the variance is always non-negative.

Provided that a regime switch is triggered by a positive variance in the model, it follows that history suggests a positive variance should be found on the dates that stabilisation programmes were introduced. This should be the case if the central bank is rational and behaves according to the assumption in section 5.3. Secondly, departures from the dates suggested by the model could be considered as coming from externalities and/or constraints faced by the central bank.

The above hypothesis will be tested using a conditional variance or volatility model for inflation. In doing so, a *general-to-specific* approach will be used for the family of conditional variance models that fall within the definition of ARCH. Specifically, an autoregressive AR(r) process for inflation, as suggested by equation (5.9), will be used, such that:

$$x_t = \beta_0 + \sum_{k=1}^{r} \beta_k x_{t-k} + \varepsilon_t \tag{5.9}$$

[8] This does not account for other forms of stabilisation, such as the unorthodox plans with which these countries have historically experimented.

where, $\varepsilon_t \sim N\left(0, \sigma_t^2\right)$. The variance of (5.9) will be tested for a $\text{ARCH}\left(q\right)$ process given by:

$$\sigma_t^2 = \xi_0 + \sum_{i=1}^{q} \xi_i \varepsilon_{t-i}^2 \tag{5.10}$$

From equations (5.9) and (5.10), it follows that condition (5.8) translates into: $Var\left(\varepsilon_t\right) \cong \sigma_t^2$.

Table 5.1: IMF stabilisation dates in a sample of selected countries

Country	Program dates/names
Argentina	1973Q3 1978Q4 (Tablita) 1985Q1 (Austral) 1990Q1 (Bonex) 1991Q2 (Convertibility)
Brazil	1986Q1 (Cruzado) 1990Q2 (Collor) 1994Q3 (Real)
Chile	1975Q2 1978Q1 (Real)
Mexico	1988Q1 1995Q1
Peru	1981Q3 1985Q4 1990Q3
Uruguay	1978Q4 (Tablita) 1991Q3

Source: International Monetary Fund.

Turning to the empirical exercise, equations (5.9) and (5.10) were individually estimated for the 6 Latin American economies presented in Table 5.1. Overall, the sample includes a total of 17 ERBS programmes as formally defined by the IMF.[9] The estimation was carried out using quarterly and seasonally adjusted data ranging from the first quarter of 1970 up to the fourth quarter of 2004. For each country, the local inflation rate (π_t) was approximated by the quarter to quarter change in the consumer price index (CPI), and the foreign inflation rate (π_t^*) by the quarter to quarter change in the United States (US) CPI.[10] All variables were taken from the IMF *International Financial Statistics* (IFS).

Before engaging in the formal econometrics, the integration properties of equation (5.9) were evaluated using the Phillips-Perron (1988) test statistic.[11] Table 5.2 shows that inflation differentials follow I(0) process in all countries in the sample. Integration was also tested for the growth of seasonally adjusted money supply (M1), which will be used later in the chapter for performing robustness tests on the conditional variance model. The results indicate that log changes in M1 are I(*0*) and consistent with the proposed model in all of the sample countries.

The first step of the exercise is to test the hypothesis that inflations in countries that have a history of stabilisation attempts are *heteroskedastic*. For this purpose, equation (5.9) was estimated for each country and several *heteroskedasticity* tests were carryout on the residuals. If the hypotheses of the model are correct, the null of no *heteroskedasticity* should be rejected against the one side alternative of *heteroskedastic* residuals. In particular, the Breusch-Pagan-Godfrey test (see Breusch-Pagan 1979; Godfrey 1978), the Harvey (1976) test, the Glejser (1969) test, the ARCH Lagrange multiplier (LM) test for autoregressive conditional *heteroskedasticity* (Engle 1982) and White's (1980), which is a test of unknown general form *heteroskedasticity*, were carried out.

[9] Available CPI data for Brazil starts in the first quarter of 1980. In Mexico, the sample starts in the first quarter of 1976 to avoid a data break in the first quarter of 1977 as a result of data overlapping (see IMF IFS report).

[10] The choice of the US CPI as a measure of foreign inflation relies on the fact that the US is considered the main trading partner for many Latin American countries and most certainly for the ones in this sample.

[11] Phillips and Perron (1988) propose an alternative nonparametric method for controlling serial correlation when testing for a unit root in the presence of lagged dependent variables.

Table 5.2: Phillips-Perron unit root test statistic for selected countries and selected variables

Variable	Argentina	Brazil	Chile	Mexico	Peru	Uruguay
p-p^*	-1.23	0.98	1.84	-0.52	-0.43	-2.00
$x = \Delta log(p) - \Delta log(p^*)$	-5.56*	-3.79*	-5.25*	-9.08*	-3.85*	-4.92*
m	-1.54	-1.68	-1.87	-1.89	-1.43	-1.36
Δm	-3.13*	-4.17*	-10.01*	-14.85*	-3.13*	-4.59*

Note: p is the local CPI and p^* is the US CPI. * and ** denote significance at the 1% and 5% level under MacKinnon (1996) one side critical surface for an intercept and no trend in the regression equation. Phillips-Perron test statistic using Newey-West and Bartlett kernel estimation. Estimation sample is 1970Q1-2004Q1. Mexico sample is 1976Q1-2004Q1 and Brazil sample is 1980Q1-2004Q1. The data is available by request to the authors.

Table 5.3: AR estimates of inflation regressions and residual heterskedasticity tests for selected counties

Coefficients	Argentina	Brazil	Chile	Mexico	Peru	Uruguay
β_o	0.03 *	0.03 *	0.01 *	0.01 *	0.03 *	0.01 *
	(1.62)	(1.44)	(1.15)	(1.94)	(1.52)	(2.00)
β_1	0.41 *	1.07 *	0.65*	0.85 *	0.62*	0.35 *
	(4.71)	(10.31)	(7.63)	(16.36)	(7.21)	(4.01)
β_2	0.19	(0.41)	0.24		0.20	0.33
	(2.12)	-2.79	(2.85)		(2.37)	(3.80)
β_3	0.21	0.22				0.17
	(2.43)	(2.12)				(1.96)
R^2	0.49	0.76	0.74	0.72	0.61	0.57
LL	31.77	44.64	180.82	208.68	47.86	252.46
N	135	95	135	107	135	135
σ_π	0.19	0.15	0.06	0.03	0.17	0.04
DW	1.96	2.08	2.08	1.99	2.00	2.01
$LM (N^*R^2)$	5.347	8.1991	8.6254	0.006	1.1656	0.8641
	(0.148)	(0.085)	(0.013)	(0.936)	(0.558)	(0.834)
Breusch-Pagan-Godfrey	41.64	80.67	67.95	57.59	68.19	4.66
	(p > 0.000)	(p > 0.000)	(p > 0.000)	(p > 0.000)	(p > 0.000)	(0.0326)
Harvey	25.77	68.51	44.84	49.88	53.99	0.61
	(p > 0.000)	(p > 0.000)	(p > 0.000)	(p > 0.000)	(p > 0.000)	(0.4377)
Glejser	73.18	121.44	134.64	108.50	140.17	5.37
	(p > 0.000)	(p > 0.000)	(p > 0.000)	(p > 0.000)	(p > 0.000)	(0.0221)
ARCH LM	123.12	51.74	49.13	17.86	36.78	51.32
	(p > 0.000)	(p > 0.000)	(p > 0.000)	(p > 0.000)	(p > 0.000)	(p > 0.000)
White	24.32	104.19	48.97	107.66	41.16	6.47
	(p > 0.000)	(p > 0.000)	(p > 0.000)	(p > 0.000)	(p > 0.000)	(0.0021)

Notes: * and ** denote significance at the 1% and 5% respectively. t-statistics in parenthesis . Estimated using OLS. In order of appearance, R^2 is coefficient of autocorrelation, LL is the value of the log likelihood function, N is the number of observations adjusted for end points, σ_π is the standard error of the regression, DW is the Durbing-Watson test statistic, and LM is the serial autocorrelation LM tests on the residuals.

The above tests are distributed χ^2 with degrees of freedom given by the number of parameters to be estimated in the mean regression. According to Engle (1982), and due to the nature of the analysis, the ARCH LM test should be the most relevant.

Table 5.3 presents the estimated regressions for each country alongside residual tests. The results of the mean equation show that inflation in all the countries are well explained by an AR(*r*) model, as indicated by the regression tests statistics. In particular, Argentina, Brazil and Uruguay follow an AR(3), Chile and Peru follow an AR(2), and Mexico follows an AR(1). Inflation persistence was high in all sample countries, as shown by the sum of lagged inflation coefficients. However, none of the countries depicted unit-roots indicating mean reversion. In addition, the Durbin-Watson statistic and the Godfrey (1988) LM tests show no signs of serial correlation, except for Chile in which the LM statistic for higher order serial correlation is significant at the 1 per cent level. Nevertheless, a Phillips and Perron (1988) test on the residuals for Chile indicated stationarity at the 1 per cent level.

Turning to the variance of the residuals, the results rejected the null of no *heteroskedasticity* in all countries confirming *heteroskedastic* inflation processes when analysed using the AR(*r*) model. The results provide a necessary but not sufficient condition in favour of the theoretical model proposed in section 5.2. Accordingly, for the sample of countries in the analysis, which have a history of stabilisation attempts, inflation was on average *heteroskedastic*.

The second step is to model *heteroskedasticity* using ARCH.[12] Table 5.4 presents the estimation of equations (5.9) and (5.10) for each individual country using maximum likelihood under the assumption that the errors in (5.9) are conditionally normal Gaussian. Again, a *general-to-specific* approach, using different inflation and ARCH lags confirmed that the conditional variance model for the inflation process is quite robust to an AR(1) in the mean equation with an ARCH(2) specification for Argentina, Brazil, Chile and Uruguay, and to an AR(1) with an ARCH(1) specification in Mexico and Peru.[13]

---

[12] A more general GARCH specification was also tested (Bollerslev 1986; Taylor 1986). The results favoured the ARCH model in all of the countries.

[13] All countries show a high degree of inflation persistence as measured by the coefficients on past inflation differentials. None of the countries depict unit roots implying that on average, inflation was subject to an implicit nominal anchor. An ADF tests on the residuals are stationary at conventional levels, providing evidence of mean reversion in all equations.

Accordingly, the significance of the ARCH indicates that volatility is relevant in all countries. Mexico, however, shows the lowest coefficient apparently because persistence has been historically high and volatility shocks do not appear to provide relevant *news* in the forecast of the variance. By and large, it seems that inflation in these countries is better explained by a conditional variance model as compared to the traditional constant variance structure.

Turning to the robustness of the model, and provided that inflation is known to be affected by measures of excess demand pressures, several additional explanatory variables were tested. In particular, the variable found most significant was the growth of seasonally adjusted money supply. A *general-to-specific* approach was used to estimate the specification given by:

$$x_t = \beta_0 + \sum_{k=1}^{r} \beta_k x_{t-k} + \sum_{l=0}^{s} \gamma_l m_{t-l} + u_t \tag{5.13}$$

where m_t is the growth of money and the variance equation is given by (5.10). Table 5.5 shows the results including this additional explanatory variable in the mean equation. It appears that money growth is significant in all equations, with lags ranging from 2 to 4 quarters, and coefficients ranging from 0.07 in Argentina to 0.72 in Peru. The most important conclusion derived from the results, however, is that the conditional variance remains unaffected by the inclusion of this variable confirming the robustness of the ARCH specification.

The third step in assessing the relevance of the proposed hypothesis involves determining whether the evolution of the ARCH series coincides with the dates in which these countries introduced stabilisation programmes. Figures 5.2a –5.2e compare the ARCH against actual dates of stabilisation and rolling sample standard errors for each country.[14]

---

[14] The ARCH series are drawn from Table 5.4. However, similar results are obtained if the specification in Table 5.5 is used. The rolling standard errors are based on sub-sample periods that run from one stabilisation episode to the next. This is to have a statistical base for determining when the ARCH is statistically different from zero. Although not formally derived, it is assumed that when volatility exceeds the average ARCH of the stabilisation period, volatility shocks are expected to kick-in and may signal the need to engage in a stabilisation attempt. These rolling standard errors are displayed as the staggered lines that run alongside the ARCH series in the graphs.

Table 5.4: ARCH estimates of inflation regressions for selected countries

Coefficients	Argentina	Brazil	Chile	Mexico	Peru	Uruguay
β_o	-1.2E-03 *	2.3E-03 *	1.4E-03 *	2.7E-03 *	3.1E-03 *	-3.5E-03 *
	(0.52)	(0.46)	(1.13)	(0.68)	(3.43)	2.21
β_1	0.98 *	0.96 *	0.81 *	0.89 *	0.80 *	0.97 *
	(70.53)	(48.61)	(24.51)	(18.15)	(48.47)	(78.61)
ξ_0	9.2E-05 *	3.3E-04 *	6.41E-05 *	3.0E-04 *	5.54E-05 *	8.83E-05 *
	(2.25)	(5.32)	(2.61)	(6.89)	(2.55)	(2.22)
ξ_1	1.88 *	0.60 *	1.17 *	0.89 *	2.71 *	0.76 *
	(6.05)	(2.34)	(4.78)	(3.38)	(7.17)	(2.68)
ξ_2	0.79 *	1.37 *	0.76 *			1.55 *
	(6.74)	(2.85)	(6.50)			(6.58)
R^2	0.31	0.73	0.70	0.70	0.58	0.39
LL	178.35	125.29	300.39	238.07	263.66	269.94
N	135	95	135	107	135	135
σ_π	0.22	2.35	0.07	0.04	0.18	0.04
DW	2.82	1.77	2.21	2.02	2.32	2.92
ADF-PP	-12.72	-8.46	-11.4	-10.45	-13.83	-19.66

Notes: * and ** denote significance at the 1% and 5% respectively. z-statistics in parenthesis (see Harvey (1990) for a description). Estimated using maximum likelihood with Bollerslev and Wooldrige (1992) robust standard errors & covariance. In order of appearance, R^2 is coefficient of autocorrelation, LL is the value of the log likelihood function, N is the number of observations adjusted for end points, σ_π is the standard error of the regression, DW is the Durbin-Watson test statistic, and ADF is the augmented Dickey and Fuller (1979) test for unit roots.

Table 5.5: ARCH estimates of inflation regressions including money growth for selected countries

Coefficients	Argentina	Brazil	Chile	Mexico	Peru	Uruguay
β_o	-1.7E-03*	1.8E-03*	-5.5E-04*	-4.1E-03*	-1.6E-02*	-2.9E-03*
	(1.70)	(70,183.33)	0.32	2.04	1.17	1.34
β_1	0.95*	0.98*	0.65*	0.75*	0.39*	0.67*
	(29.33)	(84.06)	(20.21)	(18.33)	(2.68)	(16.30)
γ_0	0.02	0.04	0.01	0.03	0.72	0.06
	(2.90)	(84.06)	(0.51)	(3.69)	(3.57)	(4.58)
γ_1	0.04	(0.00)	(0.01)	0.12		0.06
	(3.42)	(0.43)	(1.30)	(9.69)		(5.93)
γ_2	(0.03)	(0.02)	0.03			0.07
	(2.01)	(4.45)	(3.65)			(6.80)
γ_3	0.04	0.05	0.04			0.07
	(2.73)	(14.41)	(4.88)			(5.39)
γ_4		(0.04)	0.04			
		(15.54)	(2.85)			
$\Sigma\gamma$	0.07	0.03	0.10	0.15	0.72	0.26
ξ_0	1.9E-06*	-1.6E-05*	4.08E-05*	1.1E-04*	2.34E-03*	5.07E-05*
	(0.14)	6,704.16	(2.50)	(2.74)	(3.69)	(1.13)
ξ_1	2.24*	0.26*	0.76*	1.47*	1.14*	0.58*
	(6.32)	(2.35)	(3.26)	(3.91)	(3.71)	(2.24)
ξ_2	0.79*	3.58*	1.21*			1.64*
	(6.00)	(3.72)	(6.13)			(5.20)
R^2	0.31	0.72	0.69	0.74	0.84	0.48
LL	192.37	145.36	308.98	263.92	157.79	281.07
N	135	95	135	107	135	135
σ_π	0.23	2.29	0.07	0.03	0.11	0.04
DW	8.31	27.28	32.66	62.82	176.55	16.45
ADF-PP	-12.35	-8.17	-11.79	-8.31	-13.97	-16.65

Notes: * and ** denote significance at the 1% and 5% respectively. z-statistics in parenthesis (see Harvey (1990) for a description). Estimated using maximum likelihood with Bollerslev and Wooldrige (1992) robust standard errors & covariance. In order of appearance, R^2 is coefficient of autocorrelation, LL is the value of the log likelihood function, N is the number of observations adjusted for end points, σ_π is the standard error of the regression, DW is the Durbin-Watson test statistic, and ADF is the augmented Dickey and Fuller (1979) test for unit roots.

At first, overshooting of the conditional variance coincides with almost all of the major stabilisation attempts around the time of substantial macroeconomic volatility. The most relevant episodes were the *Bonex* plan in Argentina at the beginning of the 1990s, the Brazilian *Collor* and *Real* plans in 1990 and 1994, the hyperinflations in Chile and Mexico during the 1970s, the 1990 inflation crisis in Peru, and the high degree of persistence in Uruguay with several spikes in 1973, 1983 and 2003.

For the sample under scrutiny, the ARCH coincides with the entire set of stabilisation programmes that the literature has considered as successful. More interesting, however, is that the ARCH is uncorrelated with those stabilisation programmes that the literature has found as failed or overly delayed (see Hamann 2001).

In particular, the *Tablitas* and *Convertibility* plans in Argentina, the *Collor* and *Real* plans in Brazil, and Peru's 1985 and 1990 ERBS programmes, are cases in which the programmes are considered as fail attempts. It must be noted that overshooting of the conditional variance in the context of this model is analogous to Dornbusch's (1976) exchange rate overshooting. This can be demonstrated by using the traditional definition of the real exchange rate index:

$$\log(F_t) = s_t + x_t \tag{5.11}$$

where $\log(F_t)$ is a log-linear operator and F_t F_t is the nominal "spot" exchange rate. Using equations (5.5) and (5.6), it follows that:

$$\log(F_t) = 2\frac{\lambda}{1+\lambda}\varepsilon_t + \frac{\lambda-1}{1+\lambda}x_{t-1} \tag{5.12}$$

If *purchasing power parity* (PPP) is assumed to hold in equation (5.2), it then follows that:

$$Var\left[\log(F_t)\right] = Var(\varepsilon_t) \tag{5.13}$$

which shows that if the nominal "spot" exchange rates overshoots, it must be due to the $Var(\varepsilon_t)$.

Figure 5.2a: Regime-switching rule in Argentina

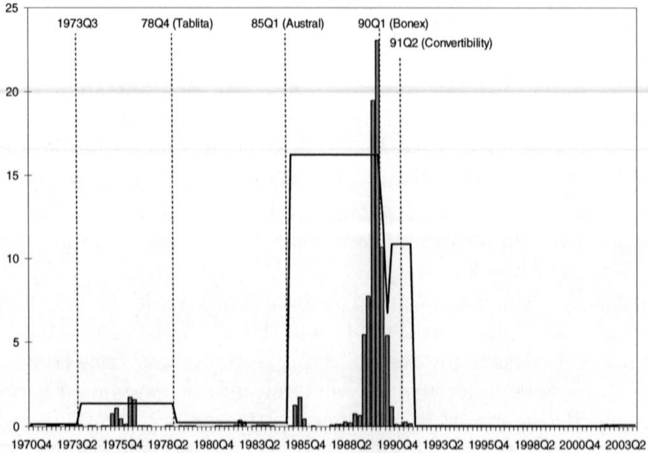

Figure 5.2b: Regime-switching rule in Brazil

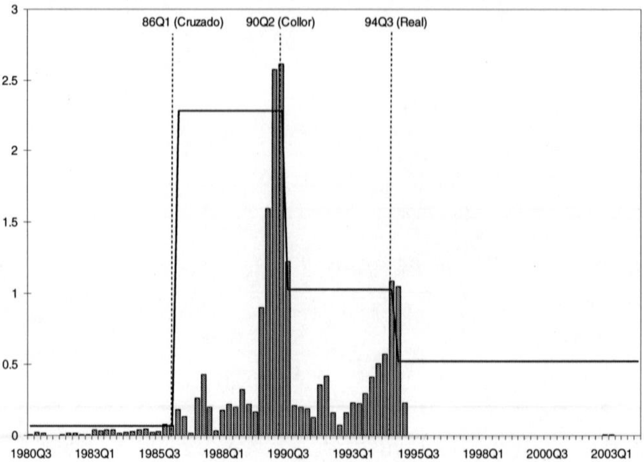

Figure 5.2c: Regime-switching rule in Chile

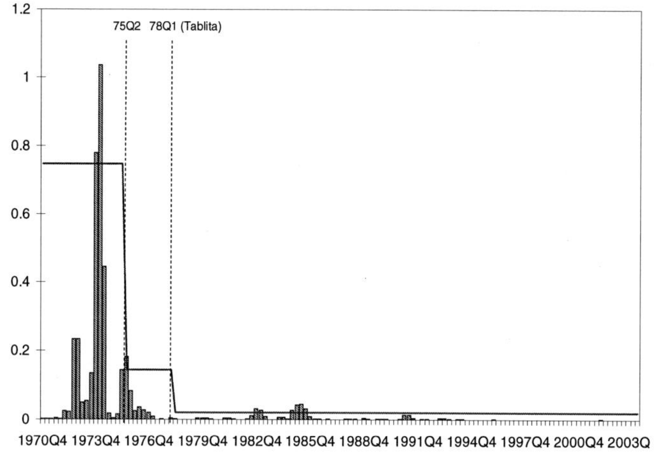

Figure 5.2d: Regime-switching rule in Mexico

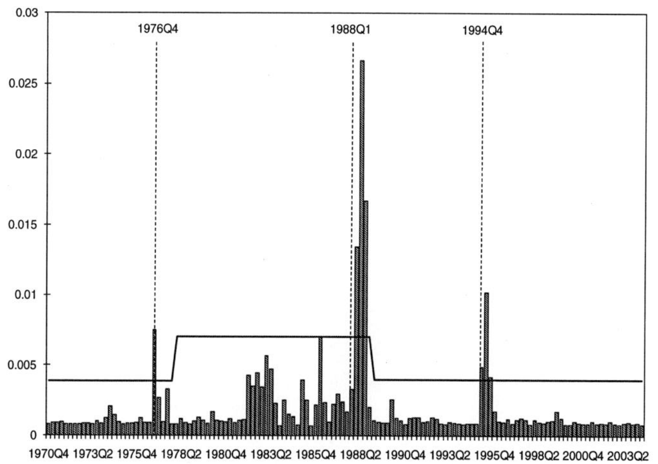

Figure 5.2e: Regime-switching rule in Peru

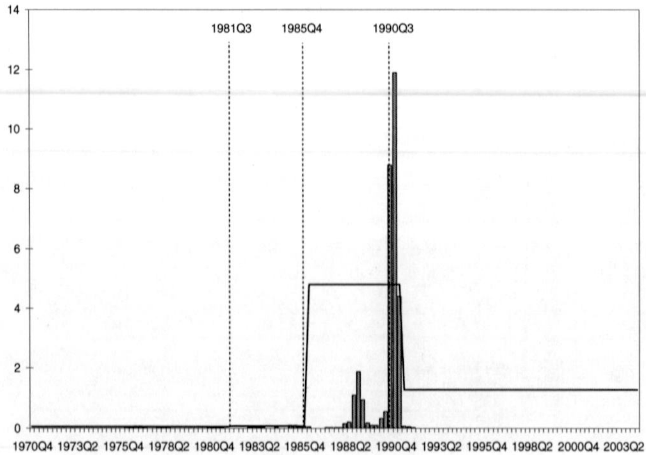

Figure 5.2f: Regime switching-rule in Uruguay

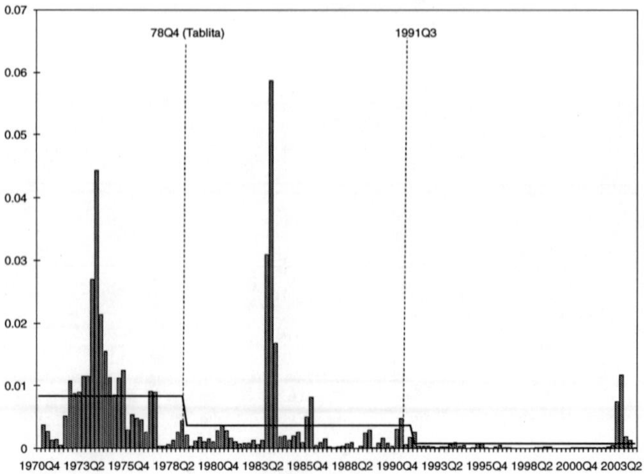

Duration in Stabilisation

This section attempts to measure duration in stabilisation using the conditional variance model as a threshold definition of high and low inflation. These threshold definitions are compared to the actual date on which the stabilisation programme was introduced. Any departures from the thresholds are understood as measures of duration producing delays in the implementation and/or in achieving stabilisation.[15]

The standard approach for measuring duration in the literature is by the difference between the actual date of stabilisation and the date the economy reaches some threshold definition of high inflation. Ball (1994) and Easterly (1996) have used rules for defining stabilisation episodes. In particular, and building upon earlier work by Bruno and Easterly (1995), Easterly (1996), ETA henceforward defines an *inflation crisis* as a period of two consecutive years of inflation above 40 per cent. In the same way, a *stabilisation episode* is defined as a movement from an inflation crisis to stability, the latter marked by a period of at least two consecutive years with inflation below 40 per cent. The two-year minimum is used to eliminate spikes in inflation due to purely one-time price shocks such as changes in import prices, exchange rate movements, and or trade liberalization.

To establish the timing of stabilisations, ETA defines the peak year during the crisis as the stabilisation year and the year after the peak as the first post-stabilisation year. ETA found 28 stabilisation episodes, although this rule could be considered a relatively stringent criterion for the selection of *stabilisation episodes*. Notably, the list excludes a number of well documented, albeit mostly failed, stabilisation attempts, including Argentina and Chile's *Tablitas* of the late 1970s, as well as the heterodox programmes of Argentina, Brazil and Peru of the mid-1980s. The sample also excludes several programmes in Africa.

In a deliberate attempt to produce a larger sample, three alternative rules were tested by Hamann (2001) to identify stabilisation episodes. All the rules are based on the requirement that, prior to stabilisation, inflation remained at or above 40 per cent for at least two years. In the first criterion, stabilisation occurs when inflation is brought down below 40 per cent and remains at that level for at least another year.

[15] The literature dealing with duration in stabilisation focuses on the externalities and political games that cause governments to delay stabilisation and/or to implement soft programmes that ultimately fail (see Sturzenegger and Tommasi 1998).

In the second criterion, stabilisation occurs when the inflation rate is below 40 per cent by at least one-quarter the first year and remains below the pre-stabilisation level for at least another year. In the third and final criterion, stabilisation occurs when the inflation rate is below 40 per cent by at least half of the first year and remains below the pre-stabilisation level for at least another year. Hamann (2001) found 34 stabilisation episodes under criterion 1, out of which 22 coincide with those in the ETA sample.

The timing of stabilisation, however, tends to be delayed by a year in most cases reflecting the fact that ETA's selection was based on end-of-period inflation, whereas Hamann (2001) used average inflation. The fact that this rule does not produce a very large number of episodes shows the discriminating power of the 40 per cent threshold. A potential shortcoming of these criteria, however, is that they could pick up cases in which inflation may have been lowered from slightly over 40 per cent to slightly less than 40 per cent, which may not represent economically meaningful stabilisation episodes.

Unlike criterion (1), criterion (2) does not impose a uniform ceiling on post stabilisation inflation but requires a reduction of at least one-quarter in inflation in the first year of stabilisation. This proved to be a significantly less restrictive criterion as it produced 51 stabilisation episodes, including all 28 found by ETA. This criterion also captures the well-known Argentinean, Brazilian, Chilean and Peruvian episodes that are not picked up by the ETA rule. Criterion (3), which requires halving inflation to a minimum, produced 36 episodes, including 22 of the 28 identified by ETA.

This section develops a comparative analysis on duration against ETA using the conditional variance model to define the threshold definition of high and low inflation. Table 5.6 shows the calculation of duration using ETA for both *delays* as well as *stabilisation episodes*. A sample of six countries that includes the 17 ERBS programmes found in ETA was used. The results show that the average *delay* under ETA is 9.1 quarters, with a 7.0 quarters standard deviation. The country with the highest average *delay* is Brazil, followed by Argentina. The *stabilisation episode of highest duration, however,* was Brazil's Cruzado in 1986, and Peru's 1981 ERBS programme. Since the data set is quarterly, and ETA's original results were based on a yearly frequency and end-of year inflation rates, the durations calculated in Table 5.6 differ slightly from ETA original publication.

Table 5.6: Duration in stabiisation under ETA

Country	Program dates/names	Delays in stabilization ETA rule	Stabilization Episode ETA rule
Argentina	1973Q3	6	2
	1978Q4 (Tablita)	15	1
	1985Q1 (Austral)	14	1
	1990Q1 (Bonex)	11	2
	1991Q2 (Convertibility)	1	1
Brazil	1986Q1 (Cruzado)	22	1
	1990Q2 (Collor)	13	0
	1994Q3 (Real)	14	0
Chile	1975Q2	11	2
	1978Q1 (Real)	0	2
Mexico	1988Q1	5	1
	1995Q1	4	1
Peru	1981Q3	22	0
	1985Q4	10	0
	1990Q3	11	1
Uruguay	1978Q4 (Tablita)	0	3
	1991Q3	5	1
Average	Mean	9.1	1.2
SD	Standard Deviation	7.0	0.9

Note: Calculations by the authors. Numbers indicate quarters.

Table 5.7: Duration in stabilisation under ETA and CVM

Country	Program dates/names	Delays in stabilization ETA rule	Stabilization episode ETA rule	Delays in stabilization CVM rule	Stabilization episode CVM rule
Argentina	1973Q3	6	2	0	0
	1978Q4 (Tablita)	15	1	9	0
	1985Q1 (Austral)	14	1	10	0
	1990Q1 (Bonex)	11	2	1	0
	1991Q2 (Convertibility)	1	1	none	none
Brazil	1986Q1 (Cruzado)	22	1	1	0
	1990Q2 (Collor)	13	0	1	2
	1994Q3 (Real)	14	0	0	2
Chile	1975Q2	11	2	6	2
	1978Q1 (Real)	0	2	none	none
Mexico	1988Q1	5	1	0	3
	1995Q1	4	1	0	3
Peru	1981Q3	22	0	20	0
	1985Q4	10	0	3	0
	1990Q3	11	1	0	2
Uruguay	1978Q4 (Tablita)	0	3	22	0
	1991Q3	5	1	none	none
Average	Mean	9.1	1.2	4.9	1.1
SD	Standard Deviation	7.0	0.9	7.4	1.3

Note: Calculations by the authors. Numbers indicate quarters.

Table 5.7, on the other hand, calculates duration using the *conditional variance model* (CVM) and compares the results against those of ETA. Some interesting conclusions arise: Firstly, the average *delay* according to the CVM is 4.9 quarters, in contrast to the 9.1 quarters under ETA. This is a significantly lower duration when using the CVM implying that stabilisation programmes were introduced by the central bank in line with what the volatility model suggested. However, the standard errors under both methodologies are not far apart (7.5 vs. 7.1 quarters) indicating that there are errors of about seven quarters among programmes under each methodology. For this reason, the CVM will sometimes coincide with the duration implied by other frameworks.

In particular, the results show that, under the CVM, duration is substantially lower in Argentina and Brazil, somewhat lower in Chile, Mexico and Peru, and higher in Uruguay's *Tablita* of 1991. Consequently, the CVM and ETA coincide with the Mexican 1976 programme and Peru's 1981 stabilisation plan. On the contrary, the CVM suggests that neither the 1991 *Convertibility* plan in Argentina, Chile's *Real,* nor Uruguay's 1991 ERBS programmes were necessary from a welfare perspective. As a matter of fact, volatility shocks had already disappeared when these programmes were introduced.[16]

Secondly, the CVM is also used for measuring a *stabilisation episode.* The CVM determines when volatility shocks return to pre-crisis levels and thus when inflation actually stabilizes. The results show that, on average, volatility shocks disappear in about 1.0 quarter with a 1.3 quarters standard deviation after a programme is introduced.

It is interesting to see from Table 5.7, however, that many of the stabilisation programmes with long implementation *delays* show negligible durations in achieving stabilisation. The reason lies, perhaps, in that most of these programmes were introduced when inflation was already stabilized, either because the authorities implemented stabilisation policies prior to formally committing to the IMF or due to a change of government that eventually consolidated its credibility by introducing a relaxed IMF plan.[17]

Cases in which the countries introduced IMF programmes before elections were the Argentinean *Austral* of 1985, the Brazilian *Cruzado* of

---

[16] It is possible that the prospect of reaching a deal with the IMF could have brought forward the benefits from implementing the agreement. This would be in line with Sargent's (1982) views about the announcement of cost-benefits effect on credible stabilisation.

[17] The literature on political opportunisms addresses this question. For a comparison of competing views on political opportunism see Alesina et al (1997).

1986 and the Mexican 1988 programmes. For example, Stein and Streb (1998) showed how voting intentions for the 1994 Brazilian presidential campaign changed in favour of the candidate Cordoso against the popularity of President Lula after launching the *Real Plan* in July of that year. The Mexican ERBS is an example where elections occurred after the plan was launched in December 1987. In July 1988, Carlos Salinas was elected President and its strategic choice to stabilize the economy using a formal programme was supported by voters enthusiastic about the on going consumption boom following the stabilisation policies.[18]

The *Bonex* plan in Argentina, the *Collor* and *Real* plans in Brazil, and Peru's 1985 and 1990 programmes, all occurred after the countries implemented self-failed stabilisation attempts that were followed by subsequent changes of government.[19] For example, the *Bonex* plan in Argentina was launched by the newly elected government headed by Carlos Menem, and the *Collor* in Brazil was launched in March 1990 right after Fernando Collor de Melo was elected President.

Conclusions and Policy Implications

This chapter shows how policy makers engage in a stabilisation programme by looking at the variance of inflation. Relying on the historical account of countries that have undergone stabilisation episodes, the analysis suggests *heteroskedasticity* and proposes a hypothesis in which a conditional variance or volatility ARCH model for inflation could provide information about the timing and duration of stabilisation plans.

The hypothesis was tested, using time-series techniques, on a sample of 6 countries and 17 stabilisation episodes that fall within the IMF definition of ERBS. The results show that inflation rates in the sample of countries are *heteroskedastic* and that the ARCH variance is highly correlated and overshoots at or near the dates in which successful IMF programmes were implemented. Interestingly, no correlation between volatility and failed stabilisation attempts was found.

The analysis provides an alternative and more rigorous approach for measuring duration during stabilisation. Also, the analysis provides a theoretical justification for using ARCH models in the empirical evaluation of chronic inflation. The approach could be a valuable tool for policy

[18] The *Partido Revolucionario Independiente* (PRI) was Carlos Salinas' political party and responsible for the introduction of the stabilisation plan.

[19] There were many stabilisation programmes, such as the Tablitas in Argentina, Uruguay, and Chile that occurred during dictatorial regimes.

makers when deciding to engage in stabilisation attempts and could illuminate the literature dealing with duration in stabilisation.

Finally, and due to its simplicity, the use of an ARCH model as a tool for identifying the beginning of volatility that may require an adjustment of macroeconomic policy could become invaluable for policy makers. On a monthly basis, central banks and the IMF could follow the ARCH to see if it is within its rolling standard error, which may help identify concerning developments such as subtle term-of-trade shocks, changes in expectations or other macroeconomic disturbances.

References

Alesina, A., 1994, Political Models of Macroeconomic Policy and Fiscal Reforms, in: Haggard, S., and S. B. Webb, (eds.), *Voting for Reform*, Oxford University Press, 37-60.

Alesina, A., and G. Tabellini, 1990, Voting on the Budget Deficit, *The American Economic Review*, 80, 1.

Alesina, A., N. Roubini, and G. D. Cohen, 1997, *Political Cycles and the Macroeconomy,* MIT Press.

Ball, L., 1994, What Determines the Sacrifice Ratio? in: N. G. Mankiw (eds.) *Monetary Policy, NBER Studies in Business Cycles*, 29.

Bollerslev, Tim, 1986, Generalized Autoregressive Conditional Heteroskedasticity, *Journal of Econometrics*, 31, 307–327.

Bollerslev, T., and J. M. Wooldridge, 1992, Quasi-Maximum Likelihood Estimation and Inference in Dynamic Models with Time Varying Covariances, *Econometric Reviews*, 11, 143-172.

Breusch, T. S., and A. R. Pagan, 1979, A Simple Test for Heteroskedasticity and Random Coefficient Variation, *Econometrica*, 47 (5), 1287-1294.

Bruno, M., and W. Easterly, 1995, Inflation Crises and Long-Run Growth, *NBER Working Papers*, 5209, National Bureau of Economic Research.

Dickey, D. A., and W. A. Fuller, 1979, Distribution of the Estimators for Autoregressive Time Series with a Unit Root, *Journal of the American Statistical Association*, 74, 427-431.

Dornbusch, R., 1976, Expectations and Exchange Rate Dynamics, *Journal of Political Economy*, 84 (December), 1161-1176.

Drazen, A., 1996, The Political Economy of Delayed Reform, *The Journal of Policy Reform*, 1, 1, 25-46.

Easterly, W., 1996, When Is Stabilisation Expansionary? Evidence from High Inflation, *Economic Policy*, 21, 67–107.

Edwards, S., 1996, Exchange-Rate Anchors, Credibility and Inertia: A Tale of Two Crises, Chile and Mexico, *American Economic Review*, 86, 2, 176-180.

—. 1998, Two Crises: Inflationary Inertia and Credibility, *The Economic Journal*, 108, 665-80.

Engle, R. F., 1982, Autoregressive Conditional Heteroskedasticity with Estimates of the Variance of United Kingdom Inflation, *Econometrica*, 50, 4, 987-1008.

Glejser, H., 1969, A New Test for Heteroskedasticity, *Journal of American Statistical Association*, 64, 316-323.

Godfrey, L. G., 1978, Testing for Multiplicative Heteroskedasticity, *Journal of Econometrics*, 8, (2), 227-236

Godfrey, L. G., M. McAleer, and C. R. McKenzie, R. Colin, 1988, Variable Addition and LaGrange Multiplier Tests for Linear and Logarithmic Regression Models, *The Review of Economics and Statistics*, 70 (3), 492-503.

Hamman, J. A., 2001, Exchange-Rate-Based Stabilisation: A Critical Look at the Stylized Facts, *IMF Staff Papers*, 48, 1, 111-138.

Harvey, A. C., 1976, Estimating Regression Models with Multiplicative Heteroskedasticity, *Econometrica*, 44 (3), p. 461-65.

—. 1990, *The Econometric Analysis of Time Series*, 2nd edition, MIT Press.

Hendry, D. F., 1995, *Dynamic Econometrics*, Oxford University Press.

Kamin, S. B., 2001, Real Exchange Rates and Inflation in Exchange-Rate-Based Stabilisations: An Empirical Examination, *Journal of Development Economics*, 64, 237-253.

Levy-Yeyati, E., and F. Sturzenegger, 2001, Exchange Rate Regimes and Economic Performance, UTDT, CIF, Working Paper: 2/01.

MacKinnon, J. G., 1996, Numerical Distribution Functions for Unit Root and Cointegration Tests, *Journal of Applied Econometrics*, 11, 601-618.

Persson, T., and L. E. O. Svensson, 1989, Why a Stubborn Conservative Would Run a Deficit: Policy with Time-Inconsistent Preferences, *Quarterly Journal of Economics*, 104, 2.

Phillips, P. C. B., and P. Perron, 1988, Testing for a Unit Root in Time Series Regression, *Biometrika*, 75, 335-346.

Rodrik, D., 1993, The Positive Economics of Delayed Reform, *American Economic Review*, 83, 356-361.

—. 1996, Understanding Economic Policy Reform, *Journal of Economic Literature*, 34, 9-41.

Sargent, T. J., 1982, The End of Four Big Inflations, In Robert E. Hall, (eds.) *Inflation: Causes and Consequences*, University of Chicago Press, 41-98.

Stein, E. H., and J. M. Streb, 1998, Political Stabilization Cycles in High-Inflation Economies, *Journal of Development Economics*, 56, 23-36.

Sturzenegger, F., and M. Tommasi, 1998, *The Political Economy of Reforms*, MIT Press.

Taylor, S., 1986, *Modeling Financial Time Series*, New York, John Wiley & Sons.

White, H., 1980, A Heteroskedasticity-Consistent Covariance Matrix and a Direct Test for Heteroskedasticity, *Econometrica*, 48, 817-838.

Williamson, J., 1981, *Exchange Rate Rules, The Theory, Performance and Prospects of Crawling Peg*, New York: St. Martin's Press.

CHAPTER SIX

ON THE CREDIBILITY OF NOMINAL ANCHORS

Introduction

Credibility is important in designing and implementing macroeconomic policies, and particularly stabilisation programmes. As Agénor and Taylor (1992 p.547) noted "… when the public lacks confidence in the ability of politicians to carry out a newly announced stabilisation programme, disinflation becomes more difficult to achieve". If stabilisation policies lack credibility, the public will eventually recognize that the programme will not be sustained, and collectively cause it to collapse (see, for example, Auernheimer 1987; Flood 1983).[1]

As discussed before in this thesis, there is also a debate on whether *exchange-rate-based stabilisation* (ERBS) is more credible than *money-based stabilisation* (MBS). According to the literature, and owing to the visibility of the policy prescription, it is believed that ERBS will have a larger and more profound "credibility" effect than MBS (see Calvo and Vegh 1994).

Credibility on the stabilisation programme can also produce an announcement effect. The announcement effect measures the initial impact on inertia observed following the introduction of the programme and captures the perception of agents on the ex-ante ability of the authorities to stabilize inflation. The announcement effect depends on subjective issues, including the IMF reputation, the type of package being proposed, the term of the government in office, and whether it is an ending-term or newly elected political party.

The IMF is not a popular institution in many developing countries as its recipes include tax reforms and balanced budgets that will create important cuts in subsidies, affecting the majority of the electorate. As a consequence, it is possible that the announcement of an IMF package in a country suffering a macroeconomic will not have the full support of

---

[1] In Flood's (1983) model, agents' anticipation of a possible abandonment of the stabilisation programme creates a self-fulfilling process.

agents, and hence will not impact inflation inertia in the expected magnitude. This point is also related to the type of package being introduced, in which MBS are known to impose heavier restrictions on the government than ERBS.

In addition, the status of the party in power will also affect the announcement effect of the programmes. If the reputation of the government in office has deteriorated, either because they have been unsuccessful in implementing stabilisation policies, or because they have delayed the necessary policies, often recommended by the IMF, it is likely that agents will consider that the programmes will not be successful. Therefore a larger announcement effect should be observed for programmes implemented after an election in which there is a change of government than for those implemented prior to elections (see Alesina et al 1997).

The announcement effect is of relevance provided that if a positive momentum is not created at the initial stages of the programme the stabilisation strategy could be jeopardised. At the empirical level, however, the question lingers: does ERBS generate a larger announcement effect than MBS? This chapter addresses the issue using a panel of 19 countries with a history of stabilisation episodes using exchange rate-based and/or money-based anchors.

Since inflation inertia is known to be closely related to the credibility of the stabilisation programme (Agénor and Taylor 1992; Edwards 1998), the analysis evaluates, on a cross-sectional basis, the degree that each nominal anchor has on reducing inertia at the time the programme is announced. The reduction in inertia is then compared among the different nominal anchors and among different regions to see if there are regime-specific effects and region-specific characteristics linked to the stabilisation episodes.

The use of a cross-sectional framework to address the questions of credibility on different types of nominal anchors is, to my knowledge, new to the literature on stabilisation. Previous studies dealing with the issues of measuring credibility, especially during the implementation of stabilisation plans have done so for specific countries and only on ERBS programmes. Even if the changes in inertia that take place during stabilisation episodes are not entirely due to credibility, understanding and comparing these changes across a large group of countries, in different regions of the world and or different types of stabilisation strategies, is of great relevance, and should become useful for the IMF and central banks around the world. Governments, politicians and the architects of stabilisation packages can wisely use this information to improve on the design and in the negotiation of IMF supported packages.

In what remains, sections 6.2 and 6.3 lay out the time-series-cross-section framework, and explain the modelling strategy. Section 6.4 discusses the results arising from the empirical exercises. Section 6.5 concludes.

A Pooled Time Series Model for Measuring Credibility

This section explains a *pooled time-series-cross-section* model to empirically evaluate and measure the credibility effect of ERBS and MBS at the time of announcement. This is accomplished by extending Agénor and Taylor (1992) and Edwards (1998), using interaction dummy variables for measuring the changes in the regression coefficients at the time the stabilisation programme is announced. According to the literature, the coefficient changes as a result of credibility effects, and thus provides an approximation of the probability that agents attribute to the success of the programmes.

On a cross-sectional setting, inflation can be represented by the following stacked stochastic process:

$$\mathbf{x}_t = \alpha \mathbf{x}_{t-1} + \beta \mathbf{m}_t + \mathbf{v}_t \tag{6.1}$$

where $\mathbf{x}_t$, $\mathbf{m}_t$ and $\mathbf{v}_t$ are n x 1 vectors of country-specific inflation processes, excess demand and supply shock, and α and β are 1 x n coefficient vectors. In equation (6.1) the α vector measures the degree of persistence or inflation inertia, β measures the impact of excess demand pressures, which usually incorporates de-trended absorption or residuals from money demand equations, and $\mathbf{v}_t \sim N(\mathbf{0}, \mathbf{\Omega})$ is the set of error terms capturing supply-side shocks.[2]

According to the literature, the credibility of a stabilisation attempt can be approximated by the changes in the α vector at the time the stabilisation programme is announced, which is a measure of the *announcement effect* of stabilisation.[3] This conclusion is drawn from rational forward-looking models where a regime change implied by stabilisation, in which the authorities set their policy reaction so as to

---

[2] Inflation is known to be determined by three fundamental elements: Inflation persistence, excess demand pressures, and random supply-side shocks (see, for example, Dornbusch, 1976; and more recently, Dornbusch and Simonsen, 1988).

[3] The evolution over time of the α vector measured, for example, using recursive regression methods, can also provide information about the *implementation* effect of the programme.

minimize the inertial effects of the α vector, will depend on agents' perception that the programme will be maintained. This argument, pioneered by Sargent (1982), indicates that the effectiveness and side cost of stabilisation will depend a great deal on the credibility of agents, and on the ability of governments to carry forward and successfully implement stabilisation policies.

As a consequence, if a stabilisation programme is perceived as credible, persistence will fall and α will drop at the time a stabilisation programme is announced. On the contrary, if stabilisation is not credible, persistence will not be affected and α will remain invariant at the time of announcement. Consequently, the evolution of the α vector can offer relevant information about the performance of the stabilisation attempt and will provide an approximation of the probability of success attributed by agents to the stabilisation programme.

The most straightforward way to measure the *announcement* effects of stabilisation, using a cross-section framework, is by evaluating the significance and magnitude of an impact dummy variable on persistence.[4] This is achieved by performing the following regression:

$$\mathbf{x}_t = \alpha \mathbf{x}_{t-1} + \Lambda \mathbf{D} \mathbf{x}_{t-1} + \beta \mathbf{m}_t + \mathbf{v}_t \qquad (6.2)$$

where $\mathbf{D}$ is a n x n country specific stabilisation dummy matrix that takes the value of one in the year of the stabilisation programme and zero otherwise. The vector Λ measures the change in inflation persistence, which according to the literature captures the net credibility impact of stabilisation. In this regard, the larger the value of Λ, the greater the credibility of the stabilisation programme. Similarly, the smaller the value of Λ, the lower the credibility on the stabilisation package.

Note that this framework is general enough, allowing the analysis of credibility on a geographical basis and to compare the impact of alternative stabilisation anchors. This can be accomplished by restricting the sample to include selected countries within a region or by only including the type of anchor under scrutiny.

Turning to a specific nominal anchor, and the credibility impact between MBS and ERBS, the model can be extended as follows:

$$\mathbf{x}_{it} = \alpha_i \mathbf{x}_{it-1} + \Lambda_i \mathbf{D}_i \mathbf{x}_{it-1} + \beta_i \mathbf{m}_{it} + \mathbf{v}_{it} \qquad (6.3)$$

---

[4] See Obstfeld (1995) for a discussion on inflation persistence and the use of dummy variable to evaluate the impact of regime changes in inflation inertia.

where the subscript $\underline{i}$ represents the type of stabilisation being evaluated (i.e. ERBS or MBS). In this regard, $\mathbf{x}_{it}$ is the subsample vector of inflation process for the countries that have introduced either ERBS or MBS.

Following the above approach, if Λ_{ERBS} and Λ_{MBS} are statistically significant, and $\Lambda_{ERBS} > \Lambda_{MBS}$, then ERBS could be regarded as a more credible anchor than MBS. If the coefficient is not statistically different from zero, then there is no credibility impact on the specific type of anchor. If both coefficients are equal, in a statistical sense, then there is no additional credibility impact attributed to a specific nominal anchor.

Modelling Strategy

The following equation will be estimated using *pooled time-series-cross section* techniques (PTSCS):

$$\mathbf{x}_{it} = \alpha_i \mathbf{x}_{it-1} + \Lambda_i \mathbf{D}_i \mathbf{x}_{it-1} + \beta_i \mathbf{m}_{it} + \mathbf{v}_{it} \qquad (6.4)$$

In (6.4), it is expected that the α and β vectors will be positive, and that the Λ vector will be either zero or negative.

A panel of 19 countries that underwent a total of 39 stabilisation episodes, out of which 16 are ERBS and 23 MBS, was used. The countries in the sample are presented in Table 6.1, which includes 13 Latin American economies.

Annual data were used for local inflation approximated by the log change in the consumer price index (CPI), and the log change in seasonally adjusted gross domestic product (GDP) for each country. The data set ranges from 1960 to 2004, with a total of 812 unbalanced pooled observations. The set is unbalanced as there are countries with shorter sample lengths such as Brazil, Nicaragua and Zambia.

One important step in the estimation process is determining the stabilisation date. As shown in Hamann (2001) and Easterly (1996), the actual date of the stabilisation programme might differ from the date inflation is actually stabilized. If the actual dates are used (those reported by the IMF), the results will be misleading.

Table 6.1: IMF stabilization dates, anchor type and success criteria

Country	Region	Beginning Date	Stabilization Date 1, 2	Stabilization Date 3	Exchange Rate Anchor	Successful Criteria 1	Successful Criteria 2
Argentina 1	Latin America	1976	1977	1977		Yes	Yes
Argentina 2	Latin America	1980	1980		Yes		
Argentina 3	Latin America	1985	1986	1986	Yes		Yes
Argentina 4	Latin America	1991	1991	1991	Yes	Yes	Yes
Bolivia	Latin America	1985	1986	1986		Yes	Yes
Brazil 1	Latin America	1965	1966	1966	Yes	Yes	Yes
Brazil 2	Latin America	1990	1991	1991			Yes
Chile 1	Latin America	1964	1965	1965		Yes	Yes
Chile 2	Latin America	1974	1975	1976		Yes	Yes
Chile 3	Latin America	1977	1978	1978	Yes		Yes
Costa Rica	Latin America	1982	1983	1983		Yes	Yes
Dominican Republic 1	Caribbean	1985		1986			Yes
Dominican Republic 2	Caribbean	1991	1992	1992			Yes
Ecuador	Latin America	1983					
Ecuador	Latin America	1984		1984			Yes
Ecuador	Latin America	1988	1990	1990			Yes
Ecuador	Latin America	1992	1994	1994	Yes		Yes
Iceland	Other	1976	1976	1976			Yes
Iceland	Other	1983	1984	1984	Yes		Yes
Israel	Other	1985	1986	1986	Yes	Yes	Yes
Jamaica	Caribbean	1992	1993	1993			Yes
Mexico	Latin America	1983	1984				
Mexico	Latin America	1987	1989	1989	Yes		Yes
Mexico	Latin America	1995		1997	Yes		Yes
Nicaragua	Latin America	1991	1991	1992	Yes	Yes	Yes
Nigeria	Other	1990	1990				
Nigeria	Other	1993	1994	1994			Yes
Peru	Latin America	1985	1986	1986	Yes		Yes
Peru	Latin America	1990	1991	1991		Yes	Yes
Turkey	Other	1980	1981	1981			Yes
Turkey	Other	1999		2000	Yes		Yes
Uganda	Other	1981	1982				
Uganda	Other	1988	1989	1989		Yes	Yes
Uruguay	Latin America	1969	1969	1969	Yes		Yes
Uruguay	Latin America	1975	1976	1978			Yes
Uruguay	Latin America	1980	1981		Yes	Yes	Yes
Uruguay	Latin America	1990	1992		Yes	Yes	Yes
Venezuela	Latin America	1989		1990			Yes
Zambia	Other	1993	1994	1994		Yes	Yes

Sources: Haman (2001), Easterly (1996), Tornell and Velasco (1998), IFS, National Sources and calculations of the author.

As a benchmark, Table 6.1 shows the actual dates of stabilisation and those under Hamann criteria 1, and Easterly criteria 2. An average delay of one year for a stabilisation plan to succeed under both methodologies is observed. Another important aspect is that out of the 39 stabilisation episodes, only 14 are successful under Easterly, and 24 under Hamann. The exercise uses Hamann (2001) criteria 2 as the dates for stabilisation.

Since Hamman did not include the Dominican Republic 1985, Chile 1964, Ecuador 1983 and 1984, Mexico 1995, Nigeria 1993, Turkey 1999, and Venezuela 1993, I have used his methodology to calculate the success criteria for these additional countries in an effort to expand the sample.

Cross-section Results

Table 6.3 presents the results of estimating equation (6.4) under four regression groups according to the different regions used, and two regressions per group according to ERBS and MBS programmes. The full sample includes all countries; the LATAM sample includes only the Latin American (LATAM) countries, namely Argentina, Bolivia, Brazil, Chile, Costa Rica, Dominican Republic (DR), Ecuador, Jamaica, Mexico, Nicaragua, Peru, Uruguay and Venezuela.

The NON-LATAM sample includes Israel, Iceland, Turkey, Zambia, Nigeria and Uganda, and the CA includes only the Caribbean countries namely Dominican Republic and Jamaica. In the full sample, the regressions have 52 observations, 19 cross-sections and 745 pooled unbalanced observations. The R^2 is around 94 per cent and the standar error (SE) and Durbin Watson (DW) statistics are around 0.12 and 1.3 respectively.

In the LATAM sample, the regressions have 52 observations, 13 cross-sections and 563 pooled unbalanced observations with an R^2 of around 95 per cent and the SE and DW statistics at 0.13 and 1.4 respectively. For the NON-LATAM sample, the regressions have 52 observations, 6 cross-sections and 182 pooled unbalanced observations. The R^2 is around 88 per cent and the SE and DW statistics are around 0.09 and 1.8 respectively. Finally, the CA sample has only one regression for MBS episodes with 48 observations, 2 cross-sections (DR and Jamaica) and 89 pooled observations. The R^2 is 0.84 and the SE and DW are 0.04 and 1.9 respectively.

Looking at inflation inertia, which is captured by the coefficient of lagged inflation, there does not appear to be any significant differences between levels of persistence among MBS or ERBS in all four regression groups, as measured by a Wald coefficient test. For the full sample, the Wald test cannot reject the null of equal inertial coefficients among ERBS and MBS with a $\chi(1)=1.004\ (p=0.316)$, also for the LATAM sample with a $\chi(1)=0.402\ (p=0.526)$, and for the NON-LATAM with a $\chi(1)=0.454\ (p=0.502)$. This indicates that the choice of ERBS or MBS does not necessarily depend on the level of persistence that a country has prior to the introduction of the programmes. However, there are significant differences between inertia levels among regions.

Table 6.2: Cross-country regressions on inlfation for selected sample groups

	Full Sample (ALL)		LATAM		Non-LATAM		CARIB	
	ERBS	MBS	ERBS	MBS	ERBS	MBS	ERBS	MBS
Constant	-0.039	-0.042	-0.030	-0.033	-0.044	-0.046		-0.036
	(0.005)	(0.005)	(0.006)	(0.006)	(0.011)	0.011		(0.009)
Lagged Inflation (LI)	0.206	0.223	0.185	0.201	0.470	0.446		0.505
	(0.014)	(0.015)	(0.023)	(0.035)	(0.045)	(0.044)		(0.063)
GDP Growth	0.846	0.841	0.867	0.863	0.567	0.591		0.664
	(0.015)	(0.015)	(0.020)	(0.027)	(0.045)	(0.044)		(0.059)
LI x ALL Dummy	-0.156	-0.125						
	(0.024)	(0.019)						
LI x LA Dummy			-0.147	-0.112				
			(0.047)	(0.030)				
LI x Non-LA Dummy					-0.293	-0.256		
					(0.068)	(0.068)		
LI x CARIB Dummy								-0.490
								(0.074)
Obs	52	52	52	52	52	52		48
Cross-sections	19	19	13	13	6	6		2
Pool Obs	745	745	563	563	182	182		89
R2	0.943	0.943	0.950	0.950	0.889	0.887		0.836
DW	1.319	1.436	1.272	1.419	1.788	1.738		1.928
SE	0.121	0.121	0.125	0.125	0.096	0.097		0.045

Source: Estimation of the author.

For example, the NON-LATAM and the CA regions have a much higher level of persistence as compared to the LATAM and the full sample regressions, regardless of MBS or ERBS. It appears that the countries in these regions have higher sustained levels of inflation persistence than in other parts of the world, with the CA sample having the highest. It may be that these economies have been less successful in reducing the levels of inflation persistence even after been exposed to several stabilisation episodes. None of the inertia coefficients in any of the regions or within groups exhibit a unit root, which is evidence, as expected, of mean reversion within inflation processes. However, levels above 50 per cent such as those in the CA countries are significantly high for a sample of more than 40 years at an annual frequency.

Turning to the coefficient on GDP growth, which is an approximate measure of demand pressures, there is no significant difference among stabilisation groups, although there is substantial difference among regions. For example, the impact of GDP growth is much lower in the NON-LATAM and the CA regions as compared to the full sample. The Wald test rejects the null of equal coefficients with a $\chi(1)=37.45\ (p<0.01)$ when comparing the growth coefficient of the EBRS regression for the NON-LATAM sample with the ERBS regression of the full sample. Similar results are obtained for the MBS regression and the CA region. It appears that inflation is more sensitive to growth in the LATAM countries than in the rest of the groups, although all coefficients are significant and above 55 per cent indicating the importance of demand pressures in the analysis of inflation process, at least in a cross-section setting.

This brings the analysis to the issue of credibility as measured by an impact dummy on lagged inflation. According to the theoretical rationale, if at the time the stabilisation programme is announced there is a significant fall in inertia, as measured by the impact dummy variable, the announcement was credible. In this regard, the impact dummy not only allows measuring the credibility impact but also to compare the impact among different stabilisation strategies and in different regions.

Looking at the full sample for the ERBS and MBS regressions, the impact dummy variables were negative and statistically significant, indicating that both types of programmes have a meaningful credibility effect at the time of the announcement. Comparing the credibility impact in absolute terms, however, the Wald test with a $\chi(1)=1.766\ (p=0.183)$, cannot reject the null of equal coefficients among stabilisation strategies, indicating that the magnitude by which inertia drops at the time of the announcement is similar in both regressions. However, when looking at the relative impact measuring how much inertia drops relative to its average level, the Wald test with a $\chi(1)=3.765\,(p=0.051)$, rejects the null at the 5 per cent confidence level, in favour of the one side alternative that ERBS has a substantially higher relative drop in inertia when compared to MBS (76 per cent vs. 56 per cent).[5] This confirms the conventional wisdom that ERBS has a higher credibility effect than MBS at the time of announcement.

Similar results are obtained for the LATAM group, in which the drops in inertia are negative and significant in absolute terms. In relative terms, ERBS has also a substantially higher credibility effect than MBS with a relative drop of 79 per cent vs. 56 per cent. The $\chi(1)=6.927\,(p=0.009)$ Walt test rejects the null of equal coefficients in favour of the one side alternative. In the Non-LATAM countries, however, the inertia effect is also significant and with correct sign, although, the Wald test cannot reject the null of equal coefficient among ERBS and MBS with a $\chi(1)=0.166(p=0.6836)$. In this regard, the conventional wisdom breaks down for the countries in this group although their experience only account for 3 ERBS and 5 MBS episodes.

Finally, the Caribbean experience only includes MBS episodes, which raises an interesting question regarding the size of the country and its ability to receive international support in terms of an ERBS programme from bodies such as the IMF and the World Bank. It has been criticized that the IMF only lends support for ERBS programmes to countries that have a substantially large and influential economy relative to the US and the rest of the world, as was argued during the Mexican 1988 and 1994 programmes (Stiglitz 2003).

The degree of inflation persistence in these two Caribbean countries was on average much higher than in the rest of the world, as previously highlighted, and the impact of credibility is also the highest both in absolute and relative terms when compared to the rest of the regions. For example, in absolute terms the dummy variable coefficient is -0.490, which is significantly larger [$\chi(1)=25.209\,(p<0.001)$] than the full sample MBS regression with a coefficient of -0.125. In relative terms, the drop in inertia is above 90 per cent at the time of the announcement, which

---

[5] The Wald test is performed on the ratio of the impact dummy coefficient to the coefficient of lagged inflation, which is a measure of the percentage that inertia drops at the time of announcement relative to average inertia. Average inertia in this case is measure by the inertial coefficient of lagged inflation.

is significantly higher than in the rest of the groups in which the relative drops is in the range of 55 per cent to 75 per cent.

Table 6.4 shows the persistence coefficients of both ERBS and MBS over sub-samples of ten years. The results, based on the full sample regressions, indicate that: Firstly, the impact of stabilisation on inertia was substantially higher in the 80s than in the 70s and the 90s. Back in the 70s, MBS and ERBS had a similar impact perhaps because both set of stabilisation recipes were just introduced and there were no pre-conceptions in the public's minds as to which strategy was better or more effective.

Secondly, in the 80s, in which inflation stabilisation was very common in an era of chronic inflation episodes, the impact of both anchors increased dramatically. However, the impact of ERBS was substantially higher than MBS, in line with the conventional wisdom. ERBS in the 80s, which between both types of anchors was the most popular, also had the highest coefficient in all groups and in all sub-samples. The success of ERBS during the 80s is probably the reason of its popularity and why it has received the greatest research attention.

Table 6.3: Anouncement effect over sub-samples

	ERBS		MBS
70's	-0.068	=	-0.074
80's	-0.212	>	-0.098
90's	-0.110	=	-0.120
All	-0.156	>	-0.125

Source: Estimation of the author

Finally, during the 90s, the impact on inertia of both ERBS and MBS, fell substantially, but not to the level of the 70's. As in the 70s, the 90 ERBS and MBS had about the same magnitude in terms of drops in inertia. This also contradicts the conventional wisdom of ERBS having the greatest impact. The impact gap among the nominal anchors also varied in those decades. Again, the 80's were the decade with the largest gap. There appears to be a relationship between the size, region, and level of development of the countries and the ability of a stabilisation programme to succeed in reducing inertia. It also seems that the difference in inertia depends on the popularity of the nominal anchor been pursued. This result may be capturing the apparent bias that a certain anchor may have within the sub-periods used in the analysis and not necessarily that one anchor was better in controlling inertia.

Conclusions

The analysis shows that ERBS programmes are perceived as more credible than MBS. The credibility gap is substantial among nominal anchors and among regions. The Caribbean countries display the largest impact and the non-LATAM countries the smallest.

There is a considerable degree of inflation inertia in the countries that have introduced stabilisation programmes. Inertial inflation leading to stabilisation was higher in the non-LATAM and Caribbean countries. The analysis also reveals that the credibility gap varies over time. The gap was larger during the 80s and smaller during the 70s and 90s. ERBS had a larger credibility component during the 80's coincidently when they were the most popular form of stabilisation.

From a policy perspective, it appears that countries could benefit from negotiating and implementing ERBS type programmes. However, the evidence suggests that recently the gap coming for the *announcement* effect of each type of strategy has substantially disappeared, perhaps because the architects and institutions responsible for the design and implementation of both of these types of nominal anchors have improved. In any case, it appears that looking at the potential credibility effect that an IMF supported programme has over inertia is relevant and becomes more so when the strategy implemented is in the form of an ERBS programme.

References

Agénor, P. R., and M. K. Taylor, 1992, Testing for Credibility Effects, *IMF Staff Papers*, 39 (3), 545-571.

Alesina, A., N. Roubini, and G. D. Cohen, 1997, *Political Cycles and the Macroeconomy*, MIT Press.

Auernheimer, L., 1987, On the Outcome of Inconsistent Programs under Exchange Rate and Monetary Rules, *Journal of Monetary Economics*, 19, 279-305.

Calvo, G. A., and C. A. Vegh, 1994, Inflation Stabilization and Nominal Anchors, *Contemporary Economic Policy*, 12 (April), 35-45

Dornbusch, R., 1976, Expectations and Exchange Rate Dynamics, *Journal of Political Economy*, 84 (December), 1161-1176.

Dornbusch, R., and M. H. Simonsen, 1988, Inflation Stabilization: The Role of Incomes Policy and of Monetization, in: Dornbusch, R., (eds.) *Exchange Rates and Inflation*, MIT Press.

Easterly, W., 1996, When is Stabilization Expansionary? Evidence from High Inflation, *Economic Policy*, 21, 67-107.

Edwards, S., 1998, Two Crises: Inflationary Inertia and Credibility, *The Economic Journal*, 108, 665-80.

Flood, R. P., 1983, Comment, in: Frenkel, J. F., (eds.) *Exchange Rates and International Macroeconomics*, University of Chicago Press.

Hamann, A. J., 2001, Exchange-Rate-Based Stabilization: A Critical Look at the Stylized Facts, *IMF Staff Papers*, 48 (1), 111-138.

Obstfeld, M., 1995, International Currency Experience: New Lessons and Lessons Relearned, *Brookings Papers on Economic Activity*, 1, 119-220

Sargent, T. J., 1982, The End of Four Big Inflations, in Hall, R., (eds.) *Inflation: Causes and Consequences*, University of Chicago Press, 41-98.

Stiglitz, J. E., 2003, *Globalization and its Discontent*, W. W., Norton & Company, Inc., New York.

Tornell, A., and A. Velasco, 1998, Fiscal Discipline and the Choice of a Nominal Anchor in Stabilization, *Journal of International Economics*, 46, 1-30.

CHAPTER SEVEN

CONCLUSIONS AND POLICY RECOMMENDATIONS

Introduction

This chapter summarises the conclusions and policy recommendations found in the book. The summary starts in Chapter 3, given that Chapters 1 and 2 are mainly an introduction and literature review. The object is to provide a quick approach to the main findings of my research. In doing so, the reader can find more depth and details, in whichever area is of interest, by visiting the actual chapter on the topic. The conclusions and recommendations have not been altered from those in the main text and are only aimed at giving access to key points of what can be found in the core chapters.

Chapter Three

This chapter finds that capital mobility and currency substitution are present in the consumption patterns of Argentina, Brazil, Dominican Republic (DR), Mexico, and Peru. The empirical analysis shows that local and foreign interest rates as well as the exchange rate play a role in consumers' portfolio allocations, as implied by the extended version of the *stochastic life cycle-permanent income* (SLCPI) with rational expectations model.

Regarding stabilisation programmes, the model provides an alternative demand-side explanation for the consumption patterns observed in the stylized facts. In particular, capital mobility and currency substitution explain more than two thirds of the variations in consumption before and after stabilisation programmes are introduced. There is also evidence of a large share of consumers who are overly sensitive to anticipated changes in income, which acording to the literature, is due to credit limitations.

From a policy perspective, the findings indicate that a weakening of the local environment relative to the rest of the world could trigger significant capital flights. If agents perceive that the currency could devalue, consumption will drop in order to increase saving in foreign assets. Hence, exchange rate expectations may initiate significant capital flights that could lead to inflation and recessions. Therefore, the model advises governments on the potential effects of negative expectations over social welfare.

The strong degree of income sensitivity found in the analysis also opens a critical door to the effectiveness of income polices. However, caution is also needed if the share of consumers regarded as financially constrained is among the low-income group. In an effort to deceive devaluation expectations, restrictive monetary policy could have larger negative welfare implications as consumers that are credit constrained will receive the largest burden affecting both income and consumption. Finally, and during times of crisis, the way stabilisation packages affect the evolution of interest rates, exchange rates and inflation will have significant different effects over consumption that may not fall within the reported stylized facts and that should be taken into consideration when evaluating the effects of stabilisation packages.

Chapter Four

This chapter proposes a framework that allows an understanding of the implications of regime changes and credibility in the evolution of inflation and the equilibrium real exchange rate during stabilisation. The analysis shows that changes in credibility, in the form of programme's success probabilities, affect inertial inflation and will influence the parameters of the equilibrium real exchange rate. Consequently, understanding credibility is crucial to evaluating the performance of the stabilisation plan. The hypothesis is empirically tested for stabilisation episodes in Chile and Mexico, using a recursive *time-varying-coefficient* (TVC) technique.

The results suggest that Chile's 1978 stabilisation effort lacked credibility in its first phase programme mainly because the central bank introduced a flexible exchange rate anchor. The programme gained credibility in a second phase, however, because it reverted to a fixed nominal anchor. On the contrary, the 1988 *Pacto* programme in Mexico had a significant credibility effect in its first phase mainly because the central bank introduced a fixed nominal anchor, although the programme lost credibility when the monetary authorities allowed the exchange rate to slide under parity. The 1995 programme in Mexico was perhaps the most successful because it maintained a fixed nominal target.

The results suggest that the way in which the central bank manages the nominal anchor under an *exchange-rate based stabilisation* (ERBS) programme will substantially affect credibility on the stabilisation attempt and hence the dynamics of inflation and the real exchange rate. Structural changes can provide important information about the performance of the stabilisation programme and if ignored, could deceive the authorities in the implementation of successful inflation and exchange rate policies.

If the central bank uses the equilibrium real exchange rate to implement inflation and exchange rate stabilisation polices, and in doing so ignores the structural changes implied by the model, the conclusions can be dramatically misleading as the equilibrium gap consistent with inflation stability can be substantially different.

To understand this argument, the real exchange rate calculated using TVC is compared with the end of sample *constant coefficient case* (CCC). The results illustrate that the equilibrium using TVC is substantially different from the CCC. This difference is more relevant during times of crisis.

In particular, after taking into consideration the TVC, the real exchange rate appears to be more depreciated than the CCC equilibrium suggested at the time the stabilisation programme was introduced. As a consequence, in order to achieve inflation stabilisation, all else equal, the real exchange rate needed to appreciate more than the CCC would have suggested. Specifically, for Mexico, the actual real exchange rate was considerably above the TVC equilibrium rate than to the CCC. For Chile, the real exchange rate was significantly below the TVC than the CCC. These findings imply a serious bias in the calculation of the equilibrium real exchange rate when the TVC is ignored.

For Mexico, equilibrium was partially achieved in the first quarter of 1991, lost again during the 1994 Tequila crisis and regained after the second quarter of 1995. For Chile, equilibrium was partially achieved when the stand-by agreement was announced in October 1990, and fully reached when the programme was formally introduced in the third quarter of 1991. Equilibrium was lost between 1993 and 1995, which, according to the TVC method, was partially restored afterwards. Although both equilibrium estimates move in a similar fashion, the equilibrium gap varies substantially depending to the methodology used. In general, structural dynamics matter in the evolution of equilibrium especially during times of substantial volatility.

Chapter Five

This chapter shows how policy makers engage in a stabilisation programme by looking at the variance of inflation. Relying on the historical account of countries that have undergone stabilisation episodes, the analysis suggests *heteroskedasticity* and proposes a hypothesis in which *a conditional variance or volatility* (ARCH) model for inflation could provide information about the timing and duration of stabilisation plans.

The hypothesis was tested, using *pooled time-series* techniques, on a sample of 6 countries and 17 stabilisation episodes that fall within the *International Monetary Fund* (IMF) definition of ERBS. The results show that inflation rates in the sample of countries are *heteroscedastic*, and that the ARCH variance is highly correlated and overshoots at or near the dates in which successful IMF programmes were implemented. Interestingly, no correlation between volatility and failed stabilisation attempts was found.

The analysis provides an alternative and more rigorous approach for measuring duration during stabilisation. Also, the analysis provides a theoretical justification for using ARCH models in the empirical evaluation of chronic inflation. The approach could be a valuable tool for policy makers when deciding to engage in stabilisation attempts and could provide some clarity to the literature dealing with duration in stabilisation.

Finally, and owing to its simplicity, the use of an ARCH model as a tool for identifying the beginning of volatility that may require an adjustment of macroeconomic policy could become invaluable for policy makers. On a monthly basis, central banks and the IMF could follow on the ARCH to see if it is within its rolling standard errors, which may help identify concerning developments such as subtle term-of-trade shocks, changes in expectations or other macroeconomic disturbances.

Chapter Six

The analysis shows that ERBS programmes are perceived as more credible than *money-based-stabilisation* (MBS). The credibility gap is substantial among nominal anchors and among regions. The Caribbean countries display the largest impact and the Non-Latin-American (NLATAM) countries the smallest.

There is a considerable degree of inflation inertia in the countries that have introduced stabilisation programmes. Inertial inflation leading to stabilisation was higher in the LATAM and Caribbean countries. The analysis also reveals that the credibility gap varies over time. The gap was larger during the 80s and smaller during the 70s and 90s. ERBS had a larger credibility component during the 80's coincidently when they were the most popular form of stabilisation.

From a policy perspective, it appears that countries could benefit from negotiating and implementing ERBS type programmes. However, the evidence suggests that recently the gap coming for the *announcement* effect of each type of strategy has substantially disappeared, perhaps because the architects and institutions responsible for the design and implementation of both of these types of nominal anchors have improved. In any case, it appears that looking at the potential credibility effect that an IMF-supported programme has over inertia is relevant, and becomes more so when the strategy implemented is in the form of an ERBS programme.

INDEX